THE

RULES

OF

LIVING WELL

Pearson

At Pearson, we have a simple mission: to help people make more of their lives through learning.

We combine innovative learning technology with trusted content and educational expertise to provide engaging and effective learning experiences that serve people wherever and whenever they are learning.

From classroom to boardroom, our curriculum materials, digital learning tools and testing programmes help to educate millions of people worldwide – more than any other private enterprise.

Every day our work helps learning flourish, and wherever learning flourishes, so do people.

To learn more, please visit us at **www.pearson.com/uk**

THE
RULES
OF
LIVING WELL

A personal code for looking
after yourself

RICHARD TEMPLAR

Pearson

Harlow, England • London • New York • Boston • San Francisco • Toronto • Sydney
Dubai • Singapore • Hong Kong • Tokyo • Seoul • Taipei • New Delhi
Cape Town • São Paulo • Mexico City • Madrid • Amsterdam • Munich • Paris • Milan

PEARSON EDUCATION LIMITED
KAO Two
KAO Park
Harlow CM17 9SR
United Kingdom
Tel: +44 (0)1279 623623
Web: www.pearson.com/uk

First edition published 2021 (print and electronic)

ISBN: 978-1-292-34939-8 (print)
       978-1-292-34940-4 (PDF)
       978-1-292-34941-1 (ePub)

British Library Cataloguing-in-Publication Data
A catalogue record for the print edition is available from the British Library

Library of Congress Cataloging-in-Publication Data
A catalog record for the print edition is available from the Library of Congress

10 9 8 7 6 5 4 3 2 1
25 24 23 22 21

Cover design by Nick Redeyoff

Print edition typeset in 11/13, ITC Berkeley Oldstyle Pro by SPi Global
Print edition printed by Bell & Bain

NOTE THAT ANY PAGE CROSS REFERENCES REFER TO THE PRINT EDITION

Contents

Retirement 188

Challenge 210

These are the Rules 224

Author's acknowledgements

I would particularly like to thank the following people:

Hal Craze, for being *so* chilled
Andrew Green, for his forthright approach to retirement
Elie Williams for her wisdom

Introduction

How busy is your life? Most of us rush around between work, friends, school, housework, family, exercise, shopping, kids ... and where are you in all this? At the centre of your own universe I presume, but sometimes only a tiny speck at the centre, crowded out by all the other demands. And yet you can't properly fulfil any of those demands unless that vanishing speck is healthy and fit and happy. You don't just want to live. You want to live *well*.

Of course happiness is not a state you can occupy 24/7 for life. There are always ups and downs, and the good moments are all the better for their contrast with the bad ones. Permanent happiness – if it were a thing – would feel pretty much like permanent boredom I imagine. I prefer the word contentment: that allows for ups and downs but means that beneath the day-to-day concerns, you're broadly satisfied with your lot. It's an underlying state, not a surface emotion. Wellbeing, health, good living – call it what you will – it's about achieving a state where every day is the best it can be.

But even contentment is pretty hard to achieve in the conflicting and frenetic lives we lead. The modern world has a lot to answer for in terms of adding to the sum of human happiness – or failing to. But ultimately we are responsible for our own wellbeing and we can't blame it all on the twenty-first century. It's down to us to look after ourselves. Self help is the best kind. It is perfectly possible to be healthy and relaxed while all about you are losing their heads, but it's not going to happen unless you make it – unless you focus on you.

And the foundation of this contentment, this ability to live really well, is your health – in its broadest sense. For a start, you need to maintain good, robust physical health in order to make your life work for you. You need to eat the right foods, take the right exercise, relax when you can, keep your body in good condition.

No, you don't have to be an athlete, you just need to establish a sensible baseline that means you can withstand any knockbacks in terms of illness or injury and bounce back from them as quickly as possible. That baseline won't be the same as everyone else's – it will depend on your age and any underlying health issues or disabilities – but what matters is that you find the baseline that keeps *you* physically fit and resilient.

Your physical health is only the very beginning however. If you disregard your mental health, leave it to take care of itself, it's only a matter of time before you start to feel dissatisfied with life. You'll never achieve contentment unless you look after your mental health as assiduously as you nurture your physical health. Indeed it's possible to be mentally strong and to feel content with your life even without good physical health – we all decline in body to some degree as we age, and plenty of older people nevertheless live well and enjoy their lives. On the other hand, no matter how strong and athletic and fit you are, you'll never be at ease with yourself if you don't look after your mental and emotional health.

So this collection of Rules not only gives you guidelines for staying physically healthy, but also passes on my lifetime's observations of what emotionally healthy people do that the rest of us can learn from. I've watched people whose understanding of their own mental and emotional needs brought them contentment in all areas of their lives – at work, at school, as a parent, socially, and even in retirement. These people have found ways to live well despite the hurly-burly of life, so why not copy them, and adapt their lessons to our own lives?

These are not practical tips (although I might have included a couple here and there). These are guiding principles you can apply to any and every situation. They require you to look inside yourself and understand how you work, how you think, how you feel. Don't worry, it's not onerous – it's fun, interesting, enlightening. I've hugely enjoyed watching and learning all my life, and the lessons I've learnt about bringing balance into my life, being resilient, feeling confident[1] and coping with adversity have transformed me. I can honestly say I'm content in a way I never would have been without following these Rules.

This collection of Rules gives you everything you need to focus on yourself, live well and find contentment with your lot. However, there will always be other useful Rules we encounter along the way, so please feel free to share your own on my Facebook page: www.facebook.com/richardtemplar. I'm always pleased to hear your Rules, and to see them shared around. After all, if we all help to look after each other, that can only be good for all of us.

Richard Templar

www.facebook.com/richardtemplar

---

[1] Hmm, maybe I already had the confidence thing covered actually.

BALANCE

I'm a great believer in finding a happy healthy balance in all areas of life. It's a variation on 'moderation in everything'. You can apply it to all the areas of your life we'll be focusing on later, from exercise to parenthood, studying to retirement. You are a complex, complicated, wonderful human being with all that that entails, so you need to find space to enjoy every aspect of your life. Too much of anything leaves not enough room for something else.

It's not just about how you allocate your time of course. You need emotional balance, a balanced outlook, a balance of interests. So this section is about how to avoid being overly focused on any aspect of your life, at the expense of other areas. In fact, your time is the part that can matter least – if you're happy spending every free hour reading or jogging or playing video games, and it isn't negatively affecting anyone else, that's fine. What matters is that you're broadly content with your life. Of course there will be bad days – even bad months or occasionally years – but a good balanced approach will help you to cope with the bad times and get full value from the good times.

These Rules, about your underlying attitude to life, really underpin all the Rules that come later, and will give you the foundation you need to be as healthy and content as possible.

It's not all about you

OK, time to level with you. I know this book is called *The Rules of Living Well* but the last thing you need is to focus on yourself. That's my job, and this is the first of 100-odd Rules that are chosen to help you feel as good as possible. You, however, need to think about yourself less.[2]

I'm not trying to give you a hard time, to tell you off for putting yourself first, to criticise you for having an ego. I'm trying to help you. The fact is that people who think about themselves all the time are rarely happy. That's not just my opinion – research has shown it too. And when you consider it, that's hardly surprising. When you focus on yourself (or anything else) you're bound to start noticing the bits that aren't as you'd like – the qualities, the money, the relationships you wish you had. No one's life is perfect, and there will be things you can't change, or at least not now. The more time you spend thinking about those shortcomings, the more importance they will take on in your mind, the more touchy you'll be when you think you've been slighted or treated unfairly or overlooked.

We all know these people. They talk about themselves constantly, and if you try to steer the conversation elsewhere they just bring it back to themselves. They see everything as being about them – their boss rearranged the rota in order to punish them or get at them or make their life more difficult for some reason. Never because it was simply a more efficient system. Never because the boss wasn't thinking of them at all, but trying to balance lots of people and priorities. They can't conceive that their boss wasn't considering them personally, because they think of themselves all the time, so they have no grasp of a universe in which they're not at the centre.

Look, I want you to have the best life possible, and of course that won't work if you never consider your own needs and wants. But

---

[2] How you square that with reading this book is your problem.

to stay in balance you need to make sure you don't constantly turn your eye inwards on yourself. Understand where you fit into the bigger picture, into the rest of the world, and keep your focus outwards. That's actually where all the good stuff is.

And here's a phrase I hate: 'me-time', or 'for me'. All your time is me-time, 24 hours a day. Why aren't you spending all of it doing the things you want to? You might not enjoy them all, but in the end you do them because you want to – I dislike housework, but I don't want to live in a pigsty. I don't enjoy my kids' tantrums, but I love being a parent and the tantrums come with the package. I've had jobs I hated, but I wanted the money. I could have changed jobs, or lived on the streets, but I was choosing not to. My time, my choice. The concept of time for relaxing – which I think is behind the phrase 'me-time' – is fine in itself. Part of the problem with the phrase is that it implies the rest of your time is less good, is somehow *not* your choice, which makes it much harder to embrace all your other activities, and to acknowledge that you chose them too.

Alongside that, the phrase implies that you are more important than everyone else in your life, and the best time should be saved for your personal indulgence. That sounds to me dangerously as though the balance has slipped and you're sneaking towards centre stage. It might look inviting, but it won't make you happy.

> **TO STAY IN BALANCE YOU NEED TO MAKE SURE YOU DON'T TURN YOUR EYE INWARDS ON YOURSELF**

RULE 2

It's not all about other people

So let's balance out the last Rule with this one. While it's not all about you, you can go too far the other way and spend too much time looking at other people. What have they got? What are they up to? How are they living their lives?

It doesn't matter. Just because someone has a fancy car, or better-behaved children than you, or a job with fantastic prospects, or only seems to work three days a week, it doesn't mean their life is necessarily rosy. That car might break down constantly in the most inconvenient places. The children might be a nightmare when no one's looking, and the job might entail working in a toxic culture. They might have a tragic backstory you know nothing about. They might be battling demons of their own. There's no point envying what other people have because you're only looking at the good bits, and the whole picture might not look anything like what you expect.

Focusing on what other people have – or seem to have – isn't going to make you happy. You have to work with what you've got. You're you, and this is your life, and comparing it with other people's is futile and meaningless. It's fine to make note of what the options are to work towards. Your life now doesn't have to be your life forever – you have aspirations and ambitions to work towards. But your starting point is here, you, now. You're not starting in the same place as anyone else.

So by all means be aware of what other people have. It's fine to think, 'I'd love to go there on holiday too,' or 'I hadn't thought about working part time and spending an extra day a week with the family/gardening/sleeping.' Using what you see to inspire and motivate yourself is a great way to give you a sense of purpose. But it's not about comparing yourself with a specific person. Not least because that can far too easily turn into competing with them – quite unfair as you probably won't tell them they're in a competition. But actually unfair on yourself too, because you'll be starting behind them (you want what they already have) and you're not going to be happy until you win. So possibly not ever. And competing with other people at life is invariably sad. Winning starts to matter more than what it is you've actually won.

I've seen people end up with lives they didn't really want because they've been so busy copying or competing with other people they've forgotten to check in with themselves. For example, they compete with a sibling so much for a lifestyle that will impress their parents (are they even right about that?) that they put career before kids, or the other way round, and only notice too late that it wasn't necessarily the best choice for them.

If you're clever you'll have worked out that comparing yourself to other people is, in the end, all about you too. Well done. Not only are you focused unhealthily on what everyone else is doing, you're also turning it all back on yourself by using it as a touchstone for where *you* are – you, you, you again. This balancing stuff is tricky, isn't it?

COMPETING WITH
OTHER PEOPLE AT LIFE IS
INVARIABLY SAD

RULE 3

Look outwards

So you can't focus on yourself, and you can't compare yourself with other people. What are you supposed to be thinking about then? Well, I didn't say you can't think about other people. It's just not helpful to focus on them in relation to yourself, to compare or compete. However, if you separate yourself out of the exercise entirely and look properly outwards at others, *that* is the road to happiness, my friend.

Of all my friends who have been through dreadful experiences – bereavement, divorce, serious illness – the ones who have coped best have been the ones who have thrown themselves into looking after other people. It might be their children, it might be their work if they have a caring job, it could be friends in need, it could be charity work. It doesn't matter, because the reason it helps isn't to do with the activity itself. It helps because it keeps their focus outwards, and away from themselves.

You might think that these big traumatic life changes would be exactly the time you want to focus on yourself. That's quite under-standable, and perfectly justifiable. But we're not thinking about what's reasonable, we're thinking about what will keep you as healthy and happy as possible. And from my years of observing people, I can tell you that comes with looking outwards.

Of course it's fine, even wise, to think about where things went wrong, or what practical steps you can take, or what you can learn. If you're grieving for someone, obviously you'll want to think about them – but in moderation, not all the time. That would make you miserable and if they loved you, is that really what they'd want? Some reflection is helpful in processing and understanding your feelings. The thing you want to avoid is get-ting stuck in misery and being unable to dig yourself out.

Once you start to dwell on your troubles, that's when you set out on a downward spiral. You become unhappy or anxious or ill or depressed or several of those at once. You think about yourself and your troubles all the time, and having already been through one horrible experience, you end up putting yourself through another.

Whereas if you can find other people who can use your help, it will distract you from thinking too much about yourself. It doesn't matter if their troubles are more or less than yours on paper (it's impossible and unhelpful to compare, remember?), they will still help you to find some perspective. And it doesn't matter if one person needs lots of help, or several people can use a bit of your time. Nor does it matter whether what they need is emotional support or practical help, because what's helping *you* is having a focus outside yourself.

And on top of all that, helping other people gives your life a purpose and makes you feel worthwhile. It's great for your self-esteem, which may have taken a knock lately. That's why it beats distractions like video gaming or sport or gardening, beneficial though these can also be. It's also why you shouldn't wait until your life falls apart to try it. Helping other people should be an active part of all our lives, all the time. It makes us feel good about ourselves, without thinking about ourselves. That's a win/win.

> ONCE YOU START TO DWELL
> ON YOUR TROUBLES, THAT'S
> WHEN YOU SET OUT ON
> A DOWNWARD SPIRAL

Stay out of the sand

There's a mother I know whose teenage daughter is going through a terrible time with mental health issues. The mother can't make everything better, and she is so upset by her daughter's struggles that she distracts herself by immersing herself in her work. She has her own business so she is out of the house most of the day.

Do you reckon that's a good thing or a bad thing? Let's leave her daughter out of this – she's old enough to function independently and has her father at home if she needs an adult. I'm asking you about the mother – is it healthy or unhealthy for her to distract herself with work?

OK, that was a trick question, because we can't answer it. Only she knows the answer, and only if she's sat herself down and thought it through. The fact is that it could be healthy or it could be unhealthy, depending on how and why she does it. And that's something we all need to be aware of in comparable situations.

Distraction is an underrated strategy for a lot of things. It's a great short-term fix on those days when strong feelings threaten to overwhelm you. And it's very handy for diverting you away from pointless worry about things you can't change – how is my child's first day at school going? What if my mother's operation isn't as straightforward as the doctors expect? Did I definitely let the cat back in before I left?

On the other hand, it's definitely not healthy to distract yourself entirely from feelings that aren't going to go away. At best, it's only a matter of time before you have to address them, and at worst you'll give things time to fester or amplify so when you finally do have to face them it's even more gruelling. In other words, burying your head in the sand. You can run, but you can't hide from your feelings – they tend to pop out elsewhere, as anything from generalised anxiety to bad decisions to skin rashes. Obviously this isn't going to happen when you distract yourself from feelings of embarrassment over a minor social gaffe, say, but it is likely if you ignore strong feelings that need to be faced, that won't go away until you've dealt with them.

The answer, of course, is balance. Distract yourself from the little things that will go away if you ignore them, but don't try to run away from the important stuff that will hunt you down regardless. So be self-aware, recognise when you're using distraction as a strategy, and be realistic about whether it's a good idea. If these are feelings you have to deal with, it's still fine to distract yourself for much of the time – focus on other people, get on with life – but do also set aside some time for working through your anger, stress, grief, worry and fear. That might take hours or it might take years – it will take what it needs – and plenty of distraction will help you to cope between the evenings you sit and think, or the times you sob your heart out alone in the car, or the sessions you have with your therapist.

The real work has to take place in your head, which is why we have no idea whether the mother I mentioned is doing this or not. Only you know whether you have this balance right, and you have to take responsibility for how you deal with your feelings.

> YOU CAN RUN, BUT YOU CAN'T
> HIDE FROM YOUR FEELINGS

Follow your ups and downs

When the kids were small, my wife and I had a system for getting through those full-on days when we were all together as a family: weekends, holidays and so on. I used to take short breaks – ten minutes or so – if I started to feel the stress building up.[3] Then I could return to the fray refreshed and cheerful. She, on the other hand, never took a break. She would cope with the squabbles and tantrums and mess and noise from when the kids woke until they went to bed.

You might think that doesn't sound very fair, but she was as happy with the arrangement as I was. You see, once the children were peacefully asleep, she collapsed on a sofa and that was her day done until bedtime. Meanwhile I would load the dishwasher, tidy the kitchen, give the dog a last run ... in other words I'd make up for all those little breaks earlier in the day.

We all have our own rhythms and energy cycles. My wife was happy to keep going but, once she finally stopped, her energy sagged and she didn't want to move again. My energy works differently and, so long as I get my occasional breaks, I can happily keep going until bedtime. In fact I hate sitting still for the last couple of hours of the day, and prefer an excuse to jump up and do something every half hour or so.

If we hadn't hit on a way to make our energy levels work together so well, both of us would have found it harder work. It's important to understand your own natural highs and lows – and those of the people you live or work closely with – so you can spend more time going with the flow, and less time fighting yourself.

---

[3] Alright, alright. Sometimes she ordered me to take time out ... .

It's not only about taking breaks, of course. Some of us are morning people, or best at thinking-heavy tasks in the morning but physically more energetic later in the day. You might be most productive on a Monday, at the start of the week, or never have the energy to get up and cook a meal after a long phone call.

Once you understand these energy fluctuations – whether that energy is emotional, intellectual or physical – you can work with them. Why fight them? Schedule yourself to prepare for that sales meeting on the morning of the day before, or to walk the dog in the early evenings, or to prepare the meal before embarking on a lengthy phone call, or do 15 minutes' exercise every day rather than two long sessions a week. Of course life doesn't always work like that, and your boss won't thank you for napping at your desk all afternoon just because you're 'a morning person'. But you'd be surprised how well you can follow your ups and downs when you know what they are, and you can be more understanding with yourself when you settle for cheese and biscuits after you come off the phone to your best friend.

And remember – it doesn't matter what everyone else is doing. So what if your colleague gets into work at 8.15am every morning, or your brother spends an hour in the gym most days? Ignore all that. Just learn what works best for you and go with it as often as you can. It will make your life so much easier.

> # SPEND MORE TIME GOING WITH THE FLOW, AND LESS TIME FIGHTING YOURSELF

RULE 6

Draw tidy lines

I feel slightly uncomfortable about this Rule, since tidiness is not one of my obvious strengths, either physically or mentally, and this is not a Rule I find easy to follow. However, I do know that I feel much better when I manage to achieve it, so I'm passing it on in all humility.[4]

It's all very clever being able to multitask, but it's not actually very relaxing either for you or the people around you. There are plenty of times we have to do it – signing papers while on the phone at work, minding the kids while cooking the family meal, running over tomorrow's meeting in your head while walking the dog. All very necessary and a useful ability.

However, there are also plenty of times we don't have to do it, and actually it might be better not to. Endless studies have shown that if you do more than one thing at a time, almost invariably at least one of them suffers. And come on, you know it without needing to read the research. You're not really listening *properly* to your partner while you're checking your phone, are you?

So find a balance in your life between the time you spend multi-tasking in some way, and the time you spend concentrating on a single thing – which might be a task or a chore, or it might be a person (or dog) or an activity. It's much too easy to spend almost all your time doing several things half-heartedly, and none of them with full commitment.

So be aware of the times or activities where you know, deep down, that it would be better to focus your full attention. I know you know where these are. They have as much to do with people as with tasks – times you need to spend listening to your colleague, or playing with your kids, or making plans with your friends.

---

[4] Also not one of my obvious strengths.

Now set yourself some clear ground rules for when and how to ensure you stay focused – draw some clear lines.

Technology isn't the only distraction from these things, but it's a big part of it. So, for example, make it a rule that you don't have your phone turned on at the meal table. Or when reading to the children. Give yourself a regular hour or so with your partner of an evening when you just focus on each other, and don't jump up to deal with something else, or check your work emails. Maybe switch off everything work-related after 7pm, or make sure you never work on a Sunday, or don't think about money worries in the evenings (I know, easier said than done).

Work out which ground rules will benefit you, and benefit those people close to you. The ground rules will be different for everyone, and will shift over time, but we all need them in order to relax and stay chilled. Some of them might feel like a huge effort to begin with – especially the ones that entail not being connected to technology at all times – but if you draw them up sensibly, and stick to them, you'll soon find yourself feeling calmer and happier, and your relationships will improve along with your mood.

> YOU'RE NOT REALLY LISTENING *PROPERLY* TO YOUR PARTNER WHILE YOU'RE CHECKING YOUR PHONE, ARE YOU?

Remember what you're balancing

It's important to your general wellbeing to find balance in your everyday life, as the last few Rules show. Life is full of unpredictability – that's the fun of it – so a steady, balanced baseline gives you a healthy point to come back to every time events knock you off course a bit, as they will.

However, it's not just about your everyday life. It's all too easy to get caught up in the hurly-burly, to bounce from one day to the next as if you're in a pinball machine, to spend most of your time firefighting. On one level, when things are going well, this might be quite enjoyable. But you need to keep a weather eye on the big picture too.

This isn't something you have to think about every day, but you need to check in from time to time and assess what it is you're balancing. Are you giving the best balance of time or attention or care to the big elements of your life: work, family, friends, career? Is work going so well you've forgotten to put time into finding or maintaining a relationship? Are you spending enough time with friends? When did you last indulge your favourite hobbies? Work might be going fine, but are you making headway with your long-term career plans?

Some or all of these examples might not apply to you. You don't have to have a relationship if you don't want to, or to play golf, or to aspire to move up the career ladder. The important thing is that you make these choices deliberately, that you don't look back in 5, 10, 20 years' time and realise you should have spent more time with your parents, or applied for other jobs, or kept up with the basketball.

And the way to avoid that is to be aware of how you're balancing all the big bits of your life. Whatever works for you is fine, and you're free to cut down time in any area you wish, but for your own sake do it as a considered decision, not by accident.

To be happy most of us need variety. Not only variety of activity but also of pace. It's ideal to spend time being busy as well as time relaxing – indeed it probably makes the relaxing more enjoyable by contrast. We need time on our own and time with other people – the precise mix varies from one of us to the next – and of course time spent caring for other people. We even need a degree of stress in our lives. There are some forms of stress we'd never choose, and positive pressure is always better than negative emotional stress. Nevertheless, we need to practice dealing with negative day-to-day challenges so we're prepared when the big stuff comes along.

So do yourself a favour and keep your eye on the ball. What's it all for? What really matters to you? What do you need to stay motivated, healthy, sane? Are you spending far too much time at work, or not enough time somewhere else? If you check in frequently, you'll usually only need to make small nudges rather than big life-changes, so make it easy for yourself and monitor the big picture regularly.

> ## TO BE HAPPY MOST OF US NEED VARIETY

RULE 8

Do what you want now

How many times have you heard people say, 'When the kids leave home, we're going to go round the world' or 'Once I've saved enough money, I'm going to quit work and start my own business'? We've all done it – made plans for the long-term future. It's something to dream about and look forward to.

I read an interesting statistic recently about people building their own homes, which is a long-term plan for lots of people. Apparently, of those people who say they want to build their own home, 90 per cent never actually do it. That's quite depressing when you think about it. That's saying that 90 per cent of those people never actually get to live their dream.

So why don't they actually do it? I imagine some of them like the idea but don't quite want it enough to risk the stress when it comes to it. Others might fail to address the practicalities in terms of funding or location. Some might be overtaken by life events that make it much harder, or no longer desirable. And some may not get around to it until they feel too old to take on such a project.

But isn't that sad? I'm sure some of them move on and don't regret it, but 90 per cent? Loads of them must look back later and wish they'd done it. So why didn't they? The problem is that life sweeps you along, and the modern world is fixed on now, not some distant point in the future.

So how are you going to make sure you're not one of those 90 per cent, for whatever it is you dream of – having kids, climbing Everest, becoming a full-time musician, moving to the country, writing a book? The most obvious answer to that is not to dream of it in the future but to get on and do it now. Just do it. I appreciate it doesn't work for everything, but it is possible to take off on a boat trip round the world with your kids in tow, or resign from your handsomely paid job to become an artist. Some people manage it, so why aren't you doing that? There might be a very good reason why not and, if so, seriously considering doing it will help you realise whether actually you like having the dream but don't really want the reality. That's fine, but good to know. Not everyone is cut out to sail the world with their kids – I'd venture to suggest that most people aren't – but you might be.

Failing that, draw up a proper plan – not just a pipe-dream but a serious plan with targets and dates and everything. When will you jack in the job, how much money will you need to have put by and how will you do that? Or what kind of self-build house do you actually want and where, and what will you need to get in place to start it that you don't have now? This kind of serious planning means you can bring forward the date when you actually do the thing, instead of simply talking and fantasising about it.

You can't spend your life dreaming, but neither will you ever achieve your dreams if you don't make them happen. So keep some of them for the distant future, or just as pipe-dreams, but make sure some of them happen. Why put off until tomorrow what you can dream today?

> SERIOUS PLANNING MEANS YOU CAN BRING FORWARD THE DATE WHEN YOU ACTUALLY DO THE THING

RULE 9

Live in the past, the present and the future

Here's the ultimate balancing act. There are Rules in this book that advise you to live in the past or exhort you to be in the moment or tell you how much happier you'll be if you look to the future. The real skill is in being able to do all three and to keep them in healthy balance.

If you never considered your past you'd be unable to learn from your experiences, mistakes, successes. So of course you need to look back sometimes in order to make the most of now and of what's to come. And the past is where all your memories live, and many of those are a huge source of pleasure and comfort, even if they can sometimes be bitter-sweet. On the other hand, the past is also the home of wallowing and self-pity and guilt and shame and regret and many of the emotions that will make you miserable. So you need to visit it regularly, but be wary of the traps and don't forget how to find the exit when you need it.

We all necessarily live in the present – that's pretty unavoidable. And people who can occupy the moment fully often get the greatest pleasure out of life, because they don't worry about consequences. I remember lying on a beach when I was young and my hair was long, while the waves washed over and past me and filled my hair with sand. It took hours to wash it all out later, but I never thought about that at the time so it didn't reduce my pleasure one iota. However people who are too heavily focused on the present often struggle to cope with change, which is an unavoidable part of life. That's because they've never planned for it or prepared for it – they'd have had to look to the future to do that, and that's not their thing. And by not looking back, they make it harder to learn from their mistakes – mistakes like not preparing for the inevitability of change.

And how about people who tend to live mostly in the future? It's much easier to be optimistic here – tomorrow is always another day – and you can dream about all the wonderful things that you imagine will one day happen. You can make plans and be prepared so you're likely to see lots of your dreams come to fruition, so long as you let them. It's a cheerful, exciting place to hang out – so long as you're not prone to worry about things you can't change. The risk is that you can forget to enjoy yourself right now, in the way that when you spend ages getting the perfect photograph of a sunrise you don't actually relax and appreciate the sunrise for itself. You can't enjoy the feel of the waves washing over you while you're worrying about how to get the sand out of your hair later. And as we saw in the last Rule, if the things you really want are always in the future, you'll never actually achieve them.

So as Scrooge resolved at the end of *A Christmas Carol*, you should live in the past, the present and the future. All three of them have the ability to bring you satisfaction and joy – you just have to learn which to occupy at any given time, and know when to leave.

> # BE WARY OF THE TRAPS AND DON'T FORGET HOW TO FIND THE EXIT WHEN YOU NEED IT

CONFIDENCE

If you're going to be the happiest and most successful you can be, you'll need confidence. Confidence in who you are, in the choices you make, in the way you face the world. You don't want to go through life worrying and wondering about everything you do, every decision you make, because you're not sure of yourself.

This isn't about arrogance or complacency or over-confidence. Of course there will be plenty of occasions when you take time considering the best course of action, or wonder if you can learn anything for the future. There's nothing wrong with questioning yourself, but you want to be doing it in a spirit of healthy interest and a desire to learn, not because you lack self-belief.

Most of all, you don't need to be fretting about what other people think of you. If someone asks you to add two and two, and then mocks you when you say four, you know that's their problem. If you're naturally confident, you'll feel the same way if they choose to mock the way you dress or your accent or the way you raise your kids. So long as *you* know you've thought it through and are happy with your choices, it won't be important to your self-belief and self-esteem what anyone else thinks. Even if you listen to them (quite right too) and decide they have a valid point, you won't then question your whole personality – you'll just modify an element of your behaviour and feel grateful to have learnt something.

So the Rules that follow are designed to help you feel confident in yourself, because that underlies your ability to get the most out of everything you do at work, at home, and with your family and friends.

Your feelings are your own

Your level of confidence is largely about how other people see you – or rather, your perception of how others see you. You may not even be right about it, and indeed many people with low levels of confidence assume other people see them as stupid or useless or unattractive or incapable, when in fact that may not be what people are seeing at all. So you're judging yourself on your judgement of other people's judgement – and that's a pretty flimsy reason to feel insecure about yourself. Besides, they're probably not judging you at all – just worrying about what *you* think of *them*.

The trouble comes from allowing these supposed opinions to influence the way you feel. Even if someone tells you that you're rubbish at your job, or a bad parent, you don't have to agree with them. One friend of mine is a brilliant interior designer. If you query a design scheme of hers she'll confidently explain to you exactly why it *will* actually work. But if you were to question the way she raises her children, she'd feel miserable and inadequate. Why? Because she's confident about her work but not about her parenting skills. So that's about her, not about the other people. Many of us have this mis-match of confidence levels between different areas of our life.

You are responsible for your own feelings, no one else is. It's what you think that matters, not what they think. Whether this is a specific lack of confidence, say as a parent or at your job, or a more generalised lack of social confidence, you need to focus on your own view of yourself, independent of what anyone else thinks or says.

So ignore everyone else and decide for yourself whether you're as good at your job as you'd like to be. If not, don't feel miserable and insecure: do something about it. Think it through, adopt new strategies, ask for help, do some training, change jobs if you want to – get yourself to a point where you *know* you're good at your job, and then take responsibility for feeling confident and secure about it. Don't rely on anyone else to guide how you should feel.

That approach – identifying any shortcomings and putting them right – applies to being socially confident too. If you want to feel more self-assured, you'll have to work at it. Don't decide you're no good at it and never will be. You can teach yourself social confidence, by learning ploys and strategies, putting yourself just slightly outside your comfort zone until that feels OK and you're ready to expand the zone further.

It can also help to consider why you lack confidence. Sometimes it's rooted in the past, in the things your dad used to say to you, or the way you were bullied at school. Now you're a grown-up you can step out of those shoes and into more self-assured ones that fit you better. It's much easier to do this consciously, after analysing the root of your social insecurity.

By the way, you may already have worked out that if you can't rely on other people's poor opinions of you – real or perceived – you can't rely on their good opinions either. If people pay you compliments or admire you or show you respect that's all very nice, and I expect you'll enjoy it, but don't ever let it be a substitute for your own honest appraisal of yourself.

> # IT'S WHAT YOU THINK
> # THAT MATTERS, NOT WHAT
> # THEY THINK

RULE 11

Know yourself

The ancient Greek temple at Delphi, home of the famous oracle, had three inscriptions in the courtyard. The first of these was 'gnothe seauton' which translates as 'know thyself'. It was quoted by Socrates among many others and has an unimpeachable record for being the cornerstone of all wisdom. Kind of the ultimate Rule.

This follows on from the last Rule: you need to be able to appraise yourself honestly and unflinchingly, good or bad, in sickness and in health. If your self-image is strong, you don't need to be influenced by other people's praise or criticism. Have a clear sense of who you are – right deep down. That's not about your actions – they're just surface stuff. So it's nothing to do with whether your sales pitch was well-judged, or it was a good plan to run a charity event, or you ought to have turned up to your sister's birthday party, or the kids go to bed too late.

Knowing yourself is about the real you underneath, the one who was responsible for these actions. And how do you know who you are? You need to look at the underlying values that drive your behaviour, because in the end that's what defines you. What do you believe? What do you stand for? Some of these will seem more important than others and that's fine. Some beliefs are big – democracy, human rights, forgiveness – and some are more specific. For example, you might believe as a manager that it's important to give responsibility to everyone in your team. Occasionally this might lead to mistakes – and you'll want to analyse what went wrong and how to prevent it recurring – but you can see that the real you here was getting it right, even if the outcome might not have been what you intended.

That's why it's not about whether those surface actions and behaviours were the right ones, with hindsight. We can all make mistakes, and indeed we can all get things brilliantly right through luck rather than judgement. What counts is the values that prompted those behaviours.

I'm not giving you a blanket excuse to make rubbish decisions all the time, because if you believe in taking pride in what you do, and always being willing to learn, you won't allow that to happen. You'll forgive yourself any honest mistakes, learn from them, and do better next time. Occasionally you will even modify your values – you have to be open to that possibility if you're committed to learning and improving.

You should also be able to see that when someone criticises your actions or behaviour, this shouldn't dent your confidence in yourself, because they're not commenting on the real you. If you know yourself, and are strong and committed in your beliefs, your own opinion will be more important than anyone else's. The only criticisms that should really make you stop and think are when someone questions your values. We generally retain some of those throughout our lives, but adapt or review others when the evidence tells us to. That's real growth, because you only really evolve as a person when your values evolve.

WHAT DO YOU BELIEVE? WHAT DO YOU STAND FOR?

RULE 12

Accept your weaknesses

I can have a bit of a short fuse at times. Also I can get over-excited and interrupt people and not listen to them properly. These are weaknesses and I know they are. Oh, and also I can get into sulky moods that I'm inclined to wallow in ... We all have weaknesses. That's what makes us human.

It's no good beating yourself up about these things and imagining they make you a bad person because they don't. I know people who never lose their cool, but I don't think I'm somehow 'worse' than them. I'm probably putting in far more effort to stay calm than they are, even if I don't always succeed. Anyway, they all have other weaknesses that I don't. I might not know what those are, but I can be sure they have them because they're human.

Yes, obviously I'm working on my short temper, alright? Duh! Get off my back! Sorry ... there I go again. Look, recognising and accepting that you have weaknesses doesn't mean you blithely carry on indulging them. It's not a 'get out of jail free card'.[5] You can't simply say, 'That's the way I am' and continue to punch people in the face, or give up on everything as soon as it gets tough, or leave other people to work while you put your feet up.

We need to work on our weaknesses, to find strategies for coping with them, to apologise when they affect other people detrimentally. I've cut down my caffeine intake because, much as I love my coffee, I know that too much makes me irritable. I make a conscious effort to listen to other people even when I'm over-excited, and I actively encourage certain people to tell me if I'm becoming overbearing.[6]

So you need the honesty to acknowledge your weaknesses, and the commitment to work on them, but you also need to cut yourself

---

[5] Metaphorically or, depending on the weakness, literally.
[6] Specifically my wife. She doesn't need much encouragement.

some slack. This is just part of the human condition, and we're all in the same boat – we just have a different selection of weaknesses to contend with. Indeed, you don't have to call them weaknesses if you don't like the word. Call them challenges, or personal blips, or character glitches, if it makes you feel better. Just don't make them sound so insignificant that you ignore them.

And why is this Rule in the section about confidence? Well, it's easy to feel inadequate about your short temper or sulkiness or laziness or tendency to be thoughtless. However, confidence isn't about being perfect, and no one can surprise you with their bad opinion if you already know it's a weakness. You recognise it, you're working on it, it may not be perfect but it's a lot better than it used to be ... so they're not telling you anything you don't know already. If you're confident about it you can respond by saying, 'I apologise, I know I can be irritable at times. I'm working on it, but as you can see I'm not quite there yet.'

> **RECOGNISING AND ACCEPTING THAT YOU HAVE WEAKNESSES DOESN'T MEAN YOU BLITHELY CARRY ON INDULGING THEM**

Like yourself

If you were stuck with someone for the rest of your life – following you around, traipsing into every room after you – you'd have to learn to get along with them in order to cope. Better still enjoy their company, value them, appreciate them. Well surprise, surprise, you are stuck with someone exactly in that way, and it's you.

If you don't like yourself, don't respect yourself, your self-esteem will be low and your confidence along with it. Some people get along really well with themselves, while others find it pretty hard. A lot of that's down to innate personality, or to childhood influences, but whatever the reason it's perfectly possible to like yourself.

There's a Catch-22 you need to avoid – make sure you don't fall into the trap of believing that you don't deserve to like yourself or to be liked. That is never true, and in your case you hold the key because you have the power to change the things you consider unlikeable – not something you can do to anyone else you don't like. So work on yourself, until you like what you see.

If you're stuck in a morass of self-loathing you need a bit of distance. The thing is, we see bits of ourselves that no one else does, so it's tempting to assume that no one else has unworthy feelings or base motives. Trust me, they do. We all do. That's normal. So don't set yourself a higher bar than everyone else. Assess yourself on the basis of the bits that are visible, because that's how you're assessing everyone else.

Try to look at yourself dispassionately. Having learnt the last couple of Rules, you need an honest appraisal of yourself. But listen, if you're going to be straight about your weaknesses it's only right you should also be honest about your strengths. What are you good at? No, not maths or coding or cooking or sport. Those aren't the things we like people for. Are you a good listener, or fair-minded, or even-tempered, or considerate, or kind? Well go on then, put those things on your list of strengths.

Consider what you like and value in other people. What are the qualities you think matter to make someone worth liking? I bet you share plenty of them. Never mind motives – those are the things we mentioned that you can't see. Your friend who is always generous might only be doing it to be liked, or so that you'll be generous back, and does that matter? That is human nature, and generous is still generous, whatever the motive. So don't tell yourself other people are being genuine and you have an ulterior motive. Without going into a major digression into philosophy, everyone has an ulterior motive.

So, which bits of yourself would you not change? Start by liking at least *those* parts of yourself. Now work on the others, like we said. Give yourself credit for effort and don't get hung up on achieving perfection every time. Then like the fact that you really work at improving all the time. No, it isn't easy. Yes, it can take a lifetime. But you've got a lifetime, so you might as well get started now.

> IT'S TEMPTING TO ASSUME THAT NO ONE ELSE HAS UNWORTHY FEELINGS OR BASE MOTIVES. TRUST ME, THEY DO

RULE 14

Words can change you

I remember a school parents' evening years ago with one of my children. Several of his teachers told me – reasonably politely – that he could be lazy about his work. He had a bit of a tendency to give up if he got bored, and he was not conscientious. Mind you, they did all temper this by pointing out that as a class member he was an asset: he was laid back, easy going, didn't bear grudges.

Now, correct me if I'm wrong, but these sounded to me suspiciously like exactly the same group of character traits. When applied to his work, the teachers used negative words like 'lazy', and when applied to his social interactions they used positive words like 'laid back'. It's all a matter of perception, but you can go through life labelled as lazy, or labelled as laid back, and although they are the same trait – or at least two sides of it – it makes a big difference to how you see yourself.

Words are dangerous, and this is just one example of it. It might be your parents or your teachers or your friends who label you, or it might be you. Look how many people label themselves 'fat' when they're no such thing, and then become really miserable about how fat they are. Or consider themselves stupid when in fact they're really smart, but never got the hang of jumping through the hoops set up by the education system. So they came out of school or college with low grades and they buy into the 'stupid' label. You must know people like this who are incredibly quick-witted and sharp, but not in ways that earned them points in exams.

So if you need a confidence boost, think about the negative words that you or other people apply to you, and then find the flipside. The positive. Substitute these words in your inner monologue whenever you talk to yourself. Stop telling yourself you're lazy, and start using the term 'laid back'. Build yourself a new vocabulary where you describe yourself in positive terms.

For example, are you unreliable, or are you carefree? Are you a loner, or just someone who is comfortable with their own company? Reckless, or courageous? Fat, or just not skinny? That one's not a character trait anyway, and no reason to dislike yourself: do you dislike other people who you consider fat? Of course not (not if you're a Rules player anyway). So look, you can pick the words you describe yourself by, and then embed them in your attitude to yourself.

This is about learning to like yourself, not about giving you excuses. You can't justify any and all behaviour just by finding a word that makes it sound OK. You wouldn't say Scrooge was 'good at budgeting', or Genghis Khan was just 'single-minded'. We've already established you need to be honest with yourself, so don't find reasons to dislike yourself for qualities which are actually likeable, just because you're looking at them through a distorting lens.

> **THINK ABOUT THE NEGATIVE WORDS THAT YOU OR OTHER PEOPLE APPLY TO YOU, AND THEN FIND THE FLIPSIDE**

RULE 15

Difference is a good thing

My wife hates parties. Gatherings where everyone knows everyone else really well are fine, but big parties she hates. Don't even get her started on nightclubs and discos. When she was younger, she felt she had to go along to these things to fit in, and because it might be rude not to. She even wondered why she hated them when everyone else so clearly enjoyed them, and what was wrong with her. Fast forward a few decades and she now has the confidence, when invited to parties, to tell friends that she's just not a party person and she'd love to meet up for a coffee to see them separately. And guess what? Everyone is absolutely fine with it. It even turns out that she's not the only one who has always felt that way.

It takes confidence to be different, and open about it. And it's a shame that it takes some people years to find that confidence, and some never do. Of course it never did my wife any harm going to parties, but that's not true of all differences. Some people suffer hugely by trying to hide the things about themselves that aren't like the people around them.

Social rules are a funny thing – who decides where the line is that you shouldn't cross? Who says that you should dress or look or behave a particular way? Why does anyone worry what the neighbours will think? And why do the neighbours think? So long as you're not hurting anyone else, you're allowed to behave however you like. And the only thing stopping most of us from flaunting our differences is lack of confidence.

There's a chap near where I live – I drive past him sometimes – who always goes for a walk in full Victorian dress. Brilliant! Why can't we have more of that? Does he worry that passers-by will disapprove? Presumably not, and quite right too because I for one enjoy it. I have a friend who always sneezes as loudly as possible, and with extra optional noises added at the end. Not normally the done thing, but very entertaining. I had a teacher who used to stand on the high teacher's desk at the front of the class to declaim poetry – teachers are often known to be quite conventional so this delighted the class.

If we weren't all different, we'd all be the same. How boring would that be? It's great to be individual so don't worry about fitting in with social rules. From skipping parties to dying your hair pink, it's all good so enjoy it. Be confident – it's none of the neighbours' business (and who knows they might like it). And your behaviour might well liberate someone else to join in. Going back to the last Rule, just remember you're not weird, you're eccentric.

Of course, it's easy to say about these kinds of difference, and much harder to feel confident if you're gay in a community that doesn't accept it, or choosing to be childless in a family where everyone keeps telling you to have children, or atheist in the midst of an orthodox religious group. However hard it is, it's important to recognise that you have every right to be yourself, and other people's intolerance is no comment on who you are. The very least we can do as Rules players is to accept other people's differences. Indeed not just accept them, but embrace and celebrate them. Every one of us that does so will help those people to find life just a little bit easier.

> ## IF WE WEREN'T ALL DIFFERENT, WE'D ALL BE THE SAME. HOW BORING WOULD THAT BE?

RULE 16

Don't assume the worst

It's a facet of human nature that we see what we expect to see. If we think the world is a scary place, we'll see scary things all around us. If we think everyone is out to get us, we'll see reasons to distrust everyone. If we think people are basically good, we'll notice the good things they do – if there's any lack of clarity about their motives, we'll assume they were good. And if we think we're unlikeable, we'll interpret anything we can as evidence that someone doesn't like us. So one of the worst things about being low in confidence is that you tend to assume the least flattering interpretation of other people's behaviour towards you.

You jump to conclusions, that's what you do. Suppose someone you know quite well is getting married and you haven't been invited. If your confidence is low that will obviously be because they don't like you. What other explanation could there be? Unless maybe you're so uninteresting and insignificant they just forgot you even existed.

Or ... any one of countless other reasons you're overlooking. Maybe space is really limited. Perhaps they can't afford many guests. Maybe they did invite you and the invitation was lost in the post. Perhaps you've forgotten that you told them you hate big gatherings, or that you're planning to go abroad for the whole of August. Maybe their partner has invited your ex. I can tell you that if you were really self-confident and comfortable in your own skin, it wouldn't even occur to you that they didn't like you. So why are you thinking it? They might have been insensitive – or they might not – but the point is that there's no rational reason for it to reinforce your low confidence.

You need to question your assumptions and analyse whether they really mean what you're telling yourself they do. Is there any other interpretation you can put on this kind of behaviour? Suppose you have a friend who wasn't invited – a lovely, popular, confident, charismatic friend. Would you assume they were missed off the list because the happy couple didn't like them? No, of course you wouldn't. So clearly there can be other reasons. Now recognise those other reasons might also apply to you.

One young man I know of was invited to spend Christmas with his sister's family every year. He always felt a bit left out, because he assumed he was only invited out of duty. Eventually – prodded by a friend – he asked his sister why she kept inviting him. She replied, 'Because I love you, you idiot!' The next year he had a great time, and his sister commented on how lovely it was to see him enjoying himself, because she'd always assumed he only came out of a sense of duty.

This can arise in countless situations: someone snubs you in the street (or maybe just didn't see you?), your boss says something that could be interpreted as critical (but also could not be), you realise you haven't called your friend in weeks (but neither have they called you). In all these cases, you can assume the reason that looks worst and beat yourself up, or you can take a different interpretation. So do yourself a favour, and assume the best. You have nothing to lose, and your confidence has everything to gain. Keep thinking about your popular charismatic friend and how you would have interpreted the same behaviour towards them, if you need reminding of all the possible explanations for other people's behaviour.

WE SEE WHAT WE EXPECT TO SEE

RESILIENCE

Everything can't always go how you want it to. Life is full of ups and downs that are beyond your control. The boiler breaks down, your colleague has given you the wrong figures, the train is late, the shop has run out of milk ... and those are just the little things. Less often, but more seriously, there's illness, redundancy, bereavement, major money worries and plenty more.

If you're going to take care of yourself you can't stop these things from happening, so you'll have to focus on how you respond to them. Do they ruin your day – or your week, month, year – or do you take them in your stride? Even the worst events will leave some people devastated while others will mourn or be sad for a while but will then cope and be able to enjoy life again.

It all comes down to how resilient you are. No matter what your underlying character is, you can always improve your ability to bounce back. Yes, some people are luckier than others in their starting point, but this group of Rules shows how all of us can learn to be more resilient, more able to cope with the slings and arrows of fate, better and quicker at getting back on top of life than we used to be.

You're in charge

Sometimes fate can deal you a terrible blow. That's fate for you – nothing you can do about it. It's capricious, and if it wants to pick on you, you just have to suck it up. There are many belief systems that tell you there's no free will, and you are indeed a victim of fate. They may or may not be right, but the trouble with that attitude is that feeling like a victim isn't much fun. It leaves you vulnerable, wondering when and where the next blow will strike, and helpless to do anything about it.

It's not only the philosophers who can't agree whether we have free will or whether our lives are all down to fate. Even scientists disagree on the point. However, the scientists are clear that people who *believe* they have control tend to be happier than those who don't. If you take practical action to remedy a bad situation, you'll feel better about it regardless of whether it works. People with life-limiting or terminal diseases who 'fight' them with extreme diets or uncertain remedies may not change the outcome, but they feel stronger and more powerful for trying, and that feeling can only be a good thing.

Believing you have control and agency gives you a sense of power that you don't feel if you consider yourself a hapless victim. And that sense of power and strength will help you to feel happier and more able to cope. It might be that when you take control you can actually change the situation, which is great, but the sense of control will make you feel better regardless of whether your actions alter the outcome.

Back in the 1960s and 70s, we almost never used the word victim. Things happened that we didn't like, and sometimes other people did things they shouldn't have done – burgled our houses or called us names – but the overriding attitude was that you dealt with it and moved on, got over it, you didn't perceive yourself as a 'victim' unless you'd been on the receiving end of a serious crime.

My parents' generation never considered themselves 'war victims'. They lived through a war, with all the fear and loss and damage and disruption, and dealt with it. Of course there was a sense in which they were victims, but they wouldn't have seen it that way.

By comparison, people now are often encouraged to see themselves as victims of disasters or crimes that would not have qualified them as 'victims' 50 years ago. Words are important (as we saw in Rule 14) and the point of using the word 'victim' is that it removes any implication of guilt or complicity. Of course this is a good thing, but it's worth being aware of the flipside, which is that it also takes away any sense of power or control in coming to terms with the event afterwards. This is why the word 'survivor' is often used, because it implies more agency over your situation. Of course what matters is the way you feel, not the words you use, but the words are a useful tool to determine your outlook.

So be aware, when fate or other people treat you badly, that the more control you believe you have in recovering from the event, the more resilient you will be and the faster you will recover from the worst of it and be able to get on with your life and feel happy again. You may have been a victim at the time, but that doesn't make you helpless to respond afterwards.

> **BELIEVING YOU HAVE CONTROL AND AGENCY GIVES YOU A SENSE OF POWER**

RULE 18

You're not alone

Resilience might seem to be something that happens on the inside, some quiet, steely inner strength that enables you to recover from troubles and traumas faster than you otherwise would. There's a sense in which this is true, but it's not all on the inside. You don't have to be some kind of superhero who can handle everything all by yourself. A big part of your strength will come from outside yourself. It's about knowing how and when to call on it.

Even the most independent, self-contained person needs support occasionally, and some people need much more frequent support. Anywhere on the spectrum is fine, so long as you have the support you need when you need it. Note I said 'the support *you need*'. If you don't need it and it isn't helping, it's not support. Whether it's unwanted advice, or help you didn't need, it's just an added irritation.

Having seen in the last Rule that you need to stay in control, that includes being pro-active about who you ask for help, and what kind of help you ask for. We all need a network of people we can call on – even the strongest, most self-assured person you know has it, whether you can see it or not. And it's a network you need to construct for yourself, consciously. So, for example, that needy friend who always turns the conversation round to themselves, or gossips about everything you say to other people, is not a part of your network – not unless they're really helpful when you ask them to mind the kids, or get some shopping for you. When you need a good listener, they're not it.

Some of us rely on just a few close people, and others have a wide circle. Recognise who actually helps you to feel better or to cope more effectively, so you can get the best help when you need it. Different people are good for different things, which is why you have a range of friends. Some may be great listeners and others more practical. A friend who knows your family well will be especially helpful when you need to talk about family upsets. One who is great with kids will be just what you need when you have to stay late at work, or want advice about your child's school worries.

I'm not advising you to be needy and demanding – we all know people like that. Sometimes a natter with someone helps you to feel better and is interesting for them too, so you're not always asking people to put themselves out. And people like feeling helpful – it's good for their self-esteem – so it's fine to ask from time to time. Indeed it's fine to ask good friends for a lot in rare times of disaster, but not all the time. If you're at all concerned about being too needy, you probably aren't. In my experience overly demanding people always seem to be blissfully un-self-aware. If in doubt, there are two quick tests you can do: ask yourself if you take no for an answer graciously. If so, you're doing fine. And then ask yourself if you expect to be helped more than you help in return. If you can confidently say that you give as much as you receive – over time – then you're also fine.

After all, don't forget that you're not the only one with a strong support team. You're also part of other people's support network, and that's why it's fair, rewarding, and makes everyone feel better whether they're in asking or answering mode this time.

> YOU DON'T HAVE TO BE SOME KIND OF SUPERHERO WHO CAN HANDLE EVERYTHING ALL BY YOURSELF

RULE 19

Steel beats iron

In engineering terms, a resilient material is one that is able to return to its original shape after being subjected to stress. It's the reason why steel is better than iron in building construction, because it's more flexible in the face of strong winds, for example, and will bounce back rather than break.

When it comes to humans, we need to be similarly flexible in order to return to our original shape after being subjected to stress. In other words, we need to be prepared to give a little, to compromise, to move the goalposts, in order to come through troubles and out the other side. Most of us will more readily do this in some areas than others, and the trick is to apply it as widely as possible. For example, I'm happy to adapt a book idea into something that I can actually get published, but I have to consciously push myself to be flexible if plans to go boating get changed at the last minute.

Suppose you're determined to be a professional musician, but you can't get enough work to live on. If you persist inflexibly, living on the breadline, you're going to be miserable for a long time unless you're very lucky. Look, this doesn't mean giving in or giving up. It means not ploughing on blindly when all sense tells you that it won't work, and then being distraught when things don't turn out exactly as you envisaged. You need to re-envisage them a little bit differently, and then you can have them. So maybe make a living from teaching music, rather than performing it. Or find a different paying job, and keep performing but not for the money. You'll get the same outcome you were always going to, but you'll be much happier because you're now succeeding rather than failing. And, hey, the dream job can still happen along if you're lucky.

So learn to recognise when you're being inflexible, and inject a bit more adaptability into your approach. You probably already know where some of your points of rigidity are, so start noticing them and identifying others. Catching yourself being inflexible is a big part of overcoming it, whether it's over little things like your boss moving your desk, or big things like buying a house. Sometimes there's a good reason to stand your ground, and I'm not saying flexibility is always the right thing, but we're trying to find ways to keep you happy and healthy, and understanding when you need to adapt is a big part of that.

You'll probably realise that this is essential to making relationships resilient. Partners who aren't willing to adapt to each other aren't going to stay together. Parents who are inflexible with their children find their relationships with them suffer. Whether it's family or friends, acknowledging the need to bend a little bit makes everyone happier in the long run. To be honest, I find that letting the cat stretch the rules about sitting on my desk while I'm working ultimately makes life less stressful for both of us.

> WE NEED TO BE PREPARED TO GIVE A LITTLE, TO COMPROMISE, TO MOVE THE GOALPOSTS

Hit the off button

What's done is done. Sometimes what's done is horrible, embarrassing, traumatic, frustrating, life-changing. It's still done though, and you can't change it. You can go over and over it in your mind, you can think about how you wish things could be, you can identify exactly where it all started to go wrong ... and yet you still can't change it.

Are you making yourself happy? Of course you're not. I appreciate it's a fine line sometimes – it's worth thinking back over what happened if you can learn from it. But that's a rational exercise, not an emotional one. Once you're no longer getting any value from it, it's time to stop dwelling on the past and come back to the present, and the future.

Some people, when they get a cold, like to let everyone know how rough they're feeling. Maybe they want sympathy, or attention – which might be warranted, but the fact is that every time you have a moan to someone else, you're also reminding yourself how rough you feel. Whereas the people who insist they're fine if you suggest they seem unwell, genuinely seem to cope far better. They're accepting what they can't change, and focusing on the rest of their life.

That's easy when you have a cold, and much harder when your business has just folded, or you've had a serious accident. Nevertheless the principle is exactly the same. Overthink the past, which you can't change, and you'll feel worse. Understand its impact on you, accept it and look to the future, and you'll feel less bad.

One of the ways in which it's tempting to keep going over the past is to think 'what if ...?' Suppose I hadn't crossed the road at that moment, suppose I'd insisted on a bigger upfront payment for that huge order, suppose I'd been there when he collapsed ... This is a very typical line of thought after a calamity, accident, disaster, death. We all know it doesn't change anything, so why do we do it?

I'll tell you: it's your mind's way of trying to construct an alternative universe in which the trauma hasn't happened. It's too big to cope with, so your mind is trying to find a get-out clause. Recognising that can help you to dial down the 'what ifs'. They're not helpful in the end because you still can't change anything, and they can lead to all kinds of regret or guilt or self-recrimination that aren't fair, and certainly aren't helpful.

So learn to switch off your brain's tendency to look backwards, and to accept what has happened and work with what you've got. However much you don't want to be here, you're better off finding a way out than staying put and thinking about how unhappy you are. You don't have to deny your grief or anger or worry. But look forwards, at how you can make the best of what you do still have.

> ## ACCEPT IT AND LOOK TO THE FUTURE, AND YOU'LL FEEL LESS BAD

Be prepared

We all need help when times get rough, and the people who are most resilient are the ones who have the best ways of helping themselves at the ready. We can all count to ten when we get stung by nettles, so you need a more potent version for those scenarios where counting under your breath just doesn't cut it.

So understand yourself and know what you need in tough times, whether it's been a really stressful day at work, or whether you've just discovered your child needs a major operation. What helps? Do you recover more quickly when you're surrounded by friends, or just by one key person? Some people cope by cutting themselves off for a day or even a week to get some peace and quiet and time to think. If work is overly demanding, a quiet weekend might be the answer. If things are worse than that, a few days' holiday or a retreat might really help.

You need to know yourself, and know what works for you. And you can practise on the more manageable day-to-day stresses of life, which will not only help at the time but also prepare you for those big crises that happen to all of us sooner or later. Do you feel better for a spot of yoga, or a long soaking bath, or a natter with a friend, or going for a run, or immersing yourself in a favourite film?

There are two stages here – firstly you need to understand what helps you to cope, and secondly you need to recognise when it's time to deploy your strategies. Otherwise they're no use. Your mind will learn to associate these things with relaxing or calming down, so they'll become more helpful the more you use them.

When major disaster strikes, you can throw all your daily strategies at it and they'll certainly contribute, but a nice bath is only going to go so far when you've just discovered your partner has gambled away all your savings. So that's when you need to understand your own needs and be ready to help yourself any way you can. None of your strategies is going to solve the problem, their job is to help you manage it better.

Right. What do you need: time to yourself? People around you? Either, so long as your mother is firmly at arm's length? Does physical exercise help you to deal with things, or escapism, or meditation? Will it help to talk to a counsellor or a therapist? Do you need a day to be miserable and wallow in order to be able to wake up next morning and go at life afresh? Is there a place you can go that helps – up a mountain or by the sea or in an anonymous crowd somewhere?

Keep a wary eye too on strategies that feel as if they're helping but actually make things worse in the long run: alcohol, shopping for things you can't afford, excessive comfort eating. Know your coping weaknesses as well as your positive strategies. No one wants to go through an emotional crisis, but if you don't have these strategies ready it will be even worse, and you absolutely don't need that.

> **YOU NEED TO RECOGNISE WHEN IT'S TIME TO DEPLOY YOUR STRATEGIES. OTHERWISE THEY'RE NO USE**

RULE 22

Get it in writing

I can speak from years of experience here in saying that writing stuff down helps. I've done it for as long as I can remember. But it's not just me – research has shown that people who write down their feelings are less stressed afterwards. My habit of writing things down works because when things get emotional my head is full of thoughts and feelings that I can't properly get hold of. It's hard to make sense of them when I can't pin them down. And putting them on paper forces them to keep still and stay in one place where I can see them.

This is one of those many coping strategies I mentioned in the last Rule which can help you to cope better with grief, stress, trauma and disaster, as well as with those more short-term crises that can jump up and bite you. I've kept a journal off and on all my life since I was a teenager, and when I look back over it I can see clearly that the reason it's so off-and-on is because I never bothered to write in it when my life was going smoothly. I didn't need to. It took me a while to notice that I only wrote in it when times were emotional.

You don't have to keep a journal if it doesn't grab you. You can write down what you're feeling and then throw the paper away, or delete the document. (You can even record a voice memo and keep it or wipe it as you please.) I have a friend who always writes poetry, although funnily enough the muse only visits when she's going through emotional upheaval. I also have friends who cope with money worries by putting all their incomings and outgoings on a spreadsheet – this might sound like a different thing but it isn't. They are putting things in writing in order to make sense of their worries and feelings, as well as to keep track of the finances.

Writing things for other people to read can help because you have to explain your feelings really well for someone else. If you have a friend you can write to, either by email or old-fashioned letter, that can be really useful for expressing your feelings to yourself under the guise of telling your friend.

If you're angry or upset with a particular person, writing to them can exacerbate things. Although not if you don't send it ... Writing a letter to the person who you feel is responsible for your stress can be really cathartic. My personal rule for this is always to put it on paper and not into an email, because I can't always trust myself not to hit 'send' in the heat of the moment. Once I've written the letter, I always sit on it for 24 hours before I consider posting it. Then I re-read it and have the options to post it, edit it, bin it, or show it to a friend and consult their view. I almost invariably bin it, because it has served its purpose and I probably feel a whole lot better. I might then speak to the person directly, having both clarified my thoughts and calmed down.

Don't knock a list either. To-do lists of all kinds aren't only of practical use. They also help to clear your head if you're feeling overwhelmed or anxious, and are as much a way of coping with these difficult emotions as making sure you don't forget to pack your underwear. Sometimes their only role is emotional: lists of things you want to remember about someone who has died, reasons you love someone or should leave them, pros and cons of emotional decisions.

> **PEOPLE WHO WRITE DOWN THEIR FEELINGS ARE LESS STRESSED AFTERWARDS**

RULE 23

Weigh yourself up

If you want to be resilient, you have to understand what works for you and, just as importantly, what doesn't. As in what works for you in terms of the situations you get into, as well as how you deal with them, and your ways of coping with the emotional fall-out. The better you know yourself, the better you can look after yourself. Self-awareness is key.

If you were a recovering alcoholic, you'd know it was a smart idea to stay away from bars and pubs. Why make life more difficult for yourself? In the same way, you need to recognise as many triggers as you can for feelings you don't like – worry, sadness, anger, frustration – and either avoid them or, if that's not possible, at least ameliorate them. For example, on a day-to-day level, I know that having to call up the phone company for any reason is always stressful – I hate being on hold for 20 minutes before the conversation can even start – so unless it's an emergency I always save it for a day when I have the time and the patience for it.

I have a friend whose ex always arouses feelings of anger in her when they communicate, and especially by text. As they have a child it's not an option to avoid him, so she needs to manage both the medium and the time of their conversations in a way that minimises the impact on her emotions. If she starts texting him when she's already tired or fraught she's bound to come out of it feeling even worse. Another friend gets upset when passing a particular landmark that reminds him of his brother who died recently. Of course that can be a good thing – a release of grief is very cathartic – but it's something you want to do at the right time and with the right people around you. These are strategies that you can only use if you've thought through how your actions influence your feelings.

The easiest way to do this is to notice when you feel bad and ask yourself why. Why did that make me so angry? What's causing that unexpected lump in my throat? Why do I want to throttle this person?[7] Why can I feel my stress levels rising? Ooh, I seem to be feeling anxious – what's brought that on? Sometimes the answer will be obvious – once you've remembered to ask the question – and sometimes it might puzzle you for hours or even years (family reactions, for example, can take years to puzzle out: why do I always feel inadequate around my sister?).

If you really don't understand, ask for help – a friend, or a therapist for the big stuff – and meantime it will still help to recognise what you feel and when, even if you don't yet understand why.

Just one thing to add here: I'm not suggesting you have to justify or judge or rationalise your feelings. It's really helpful to understand them, and entirely unnecessary and pointless to subject them to logical scrutiny. They're feelings, and they just are.

> # NOTICE WHEN YOU FEEL BAD
> # AND ASK YOURSELF WHY

---

[7] For the avoidance of doubt: we only ever think this metaphorically.

Go easy

We all make mistakes. Sometimes we make horrible, cringeworthy, humiliating mistakes. We shout at someone we never meant to, or say things we shouldn't have done, or let people down by being thoughtless and self-focused. I've done it, you've done it, we've all done it. And then we feel dreadful about it afterwards – of course we do.

And sometimes we berate ourselves for what are, frankly, pretty minor errors. The kids had to skip their bedtime milk because you forgot to buy milk today (what were you thinking of?), or your colleague had to photocopy your paperwork at the last minute because you forgot you promised you'd do it for them (duh), or you're running late and now there's not enough fuel in the car because you didn't fill it up yesterday (idiot).

Whether these mistakes are big or small they were genuine accidents. If you'd done it on purpose you wouldn't be feeling bad about it now, would you? There might have been some level on which you were subconsciously aware at the time that you were making a poor decision, or that you'd regret it later, but you never consciously intended things to turn out as they have.

Of course you'll put things right, apologise genuinely, make amends. And I hope you'll make a mental note for next time in order to make sure there is no next time – always write milk on the shopping list and don't assume you'll remember, set some kind of reminder when you've promised to do something, never put off filling up the car.

So you've done what you can to make up for it, both in practical terms and in terms of soothing people's feelings, and you've done your best to make sure it doesn't happen again. What else can you do? I know! You can keep beating yourself up about it, keep telling yourself you're a dreadful person, go over and over in your mind what a stupid thing it was to do.

Why? Why would you do that? How can it possibly help, when you've already done all the things that would help? You're making this worse than it already is – which might not even have been that bad at all in the grand scheme of things. It's bound to be harder to recover from the experience if you make it worse, so just let it go. Cut yourself some slack, get a sense of proportion, go easy. You've done everything possible, and it's over. In the past. Finished. Move on.

Listen, I know this is very hard for some people, so understand this: the reason you're still beating yourself up after all those reparations isn't because of the thing you did (or didn't do). It's because you have an inherent need to beat yourself up, and this mistake gives your mind a great excuse. I have sympathy with that, and it should help if you understand where your self-flagellation[8] is coming from. We're back to understanding yourself again and this might open up a whole new rabbit hole, but at least you know which rabbit hole is which.

> # IF YOU'D DONE IT ON PURPOSE YOU WOULDN'T BE FEELING BAD ABOUT IT NOW, WOULD YOU?

---

[8] For the avoidance of doubt: we only ever do this metaphorically.

RULE 25

You think therefore you are

Your feelings are different from your thoughts, obviously. Thoughts are conscious things you can make rational sense of, while feelings are nebulous and capricious and beyond your control. You can choose what to think about, but you can't choose how you feel. Or can you?

Actually our thoughts and our feelings may be different, but they're not entirely separate. They affect each other, interlink, cross-refer. If you're *feeling* angry, you're likely to *think* about the person or situation that has angered you, perhaps to have imaginary angry conversations in your head. When you *feel* depressed you start to *think* about whether there's any point doing this, or how doing that would probably just make it worse. If you *feel* worried, you *think* about all the things that could go wrong, the bad outcomes that would justify the anxious feelings.

So it shouldn't be any huge surprise that you can make this work in the other direction too. You can use your thoughts to influence your feelings. Imagine you feel nervous before going on a fairground ride or giving a presentation or climbing a tall ladder, or whatever it is that makes you feel anxious. You tell yourself, 'It's OK, it's perfectly safe. Look, lots of other people are doing it fine. You'll enjoy it once you get there ...' Why do you talk yourself through it unless you know, on some level, that those conscious thoughts will genuinely calm your nerves? They might not remove the nerves altogether, but they'll certainly help.

That's something we tend to do very consciously when faced with a specific situation that we don't like. Some people manage to do it all the time though – and they're the optimists, the positive thinkers, the glass half-full people. It's their default setting to think the best of every situation, to focus consciously on the positive, to look on the bright side. When you ask them how they are they always tell you they're feeling great – because their feelings are listening to their answer and they instinctively feed their feelings an encouraging line.

You don't have to be born this way to be able to do it. Sure, some lucky people seem to think this way instinctively, but we can all train ourselves to do it, and it makes a massive difference to your ability to cope with everything from a bad-hair day to a major trauma. It doesn't make all the pain go away, but it enables you to cope.

Your big enemy is self-pity. This isn't about whether you deserve pity – your own or anyone else's. If the pity is warranted, then you certainly deserve to feel less miserable, and this is how to achieve it. So be ruthless about stopping yourself from thinking 'poor me', and replace those thoughts with others, reminding yourself of the good things, or how much worse it could be. Never let self-pity get a toehold.

So you can learn to use your thoughts to turn yourself into a person who feels consistently more positive than you do now. Then when times get really tough, you'll cope so much better. I've seen people lose their partner of 60 years and get through it by focusing on how lucky they've been and what they still have. Of course they're miserable, but they can weather it in a way they never could if they allowed self-pity to take hold, no matter how justified.

> OUR THOUGHTS AND
> OUR FEELINGS MAY BE
> DIFFERENT, BUT THEY'RE
> NOT ENTIRELY SEPARATE

Find the humour

You know those situations where you are on the phone to some jobsworth who is making you so angry you want to scream? Or you're trying to get from A to B and the traffic is terrible, and now the weather is terrible too, and you're late and sweaty and bedraggled and just want to cry? Or you're cooking dinner for the children and two of them are having simultaneous tantrums and the food is burning and then you discover you're out of pasta?

How do you cope without screaming or bursting into tears – or do you give in to the understandable outrush of emotion? The best way I've ever found to deal with it is by laughing. Of course, that isn't always easy at the time, so I imagine myself relating the experience to someone else later and making it as funny as possible: 'And you're not going to believe what happened next, on top of all that ...!' If you think about it, anecdotes about things going horribly wrong are a great source of humour after the event. The trick is not to wait until afterwards, but use the prospect of dining out on the anecdote to help you now.

I used to volunteer many years ago for an organisation that answered the phone to people in distress and listened to them talk.[9] And one of the things I noticed was that even people going through the most dreadful traumas seemed to cope better when they laughed at themselves. And the reason, so far as I could tell, was that in order to do it they had to take a mental step back and view themselves from someone else's perspective. It was that distance, that almost objective self-observation, that seemed to be giving them the detachment they needed to cope with their situation. I've since discovered that psychologists call this 'reframing', by which they mean looking at something in a different way, and the science does indeed back up the idea that laughing at your situation helps you to cope with it.

---

[9] Yes, that one.

We all know that laughter is great medicine – the act of laughing genuinely makes you feel better. Laughing at yourself is a more specific subset of humour in general, and it's the reframing element of it that's so valuable. It can also help you to deal with difficult people. For example, if your boss is prone to making patronising comments that infuriate you, try turning it into a game. See how many you can count in a day, or mentally allocate a 'most patronising remark of the week' award. This brings humour – and reframing – into the situation so that, although you hate the comments, some part of you is sort of hoping your boss will beat their record or say something outrageously patronising. This becomes even more entertaining if you can compete with a work colleague in the same position.

This also works well for partners, friends or siblings who have to spend time with a critical relative or self-obsessed friend. Knowing you can go home later and compare notes – 'You'll never guess what he said when we were in the kitchen ...!' – gives you the detachment that makes it much easier to cope, as well as storing up the fun of swapping stories later.

> USE THE PROSPECT OF DINING
> OUT ON THE ANECDOTE TO
> HELP YOU NOW

EXERCISE

No matter how busy your life is, finding room in it for exercise will help you cope and make you feel better. That doesn't mean you have to find the money to join a gym and be down there crunching and pressing and running and squatting every day. Nothing wrong with that if it works for you, but nothing wrong with you if it doesn't work. Or just doesn't happen.

It's easy to fall prey to the feeling that large chunks of your life must be devoted to formal exercise of some kind. But while that's certainly one option, there are lots of other ways to make exercise work for you, and not the other way around. And there are Rules worth bearing in mind even if you do run every morning before breakfast and then go to the gym for an hour after work.

Some of us just don't enjoy running or aerobics or lifting weights, and some of us would love to do it but can't find time between kids and work and running the house and looking after our ageing parents or whatever. And that's all fine. It's perfectly possible to get the exercise you need regardless of your life and your enjoyment – or other- wise – of taking exercise. You just need to approach it in the way that works for you, which is what these next few Rules are all about.

Think yourself exercised

Suppose you're part of a group of friends and family who hate anything that looks like exercise. Plenty of them are a healthy weight with enough energy, but they never put on a tracksuit or go to a gym or an exercise class. You feel differently though, because you love running. So you run for about an hour a day. Consequently you feel your exercise levels are really good and you're positive about your fitness.

Now suppose you take a job elsewhere, and make new friends and spend time with new colleagues. You continue to spend an hour a day running, of course, because you enjoy that. It turns out, however, that your new friends and colleagues all run too – which is great – but most of them also go to fitness classes or spinning sessions or spend time at the gym. You don't do any of that. All you do is run. So now how do you feel about your fitness level? Which hasn't changed at all since you used to think it was really good?

Most people measure their levels of fitness against the people around them, which is understandable but – as you can see – not actually a very accurate measure. You can go from thinking you're doing loads of exercise to thinking you're not doing enough, without changing your activity level at all. And what's more – and this is the important bit – studies have shown that the less active you believe that you are, the less healthy you are, regardless of your real activity level.

So your attitude to exercise counts for as much as the exercise itself. That doesn't mean you can spend all day slouching on the sofa telling yourself you're really fit – most of us would struggle to convince ourselves anyway – but it does mean that it's important to be positive about how you exercise. Focus on what you've achieved, and not on targets you've set yourself and then not met. Ignore what the people around you are doing. Acknowledge the exercise you get as you go about your normal day, as well as trips to gyms and classes and swimming pools. Recognise that if you're healthy and flexible enough for your age and have the energy you need, you're doing fine.

So the first Rule of exercise is don't sweat it. Don't stress and worry about whether you're doing enough, or whether it's the right kind of exercise. That's not only counter-productive but also unnecessary, because there are so many different ways of measuring exercise that it's almost impossible to say what counts as 'enough'. Lots of people out there are doing far more exercise than is necessary to keep them healthy, which is great if they're enjoying it, but you don't have to keep up with them. It's not a competition. And some of them have developed great aerobic fitness but aren't very flexible, or have excellent muscle tone but their stamina is nothing special, or need to run 10 miles a day only because they eat too many pies.

So ignore them. Do what feels right and is enjoyable, and focus on the positive. And that attitude alone will make a bigger difference than a few extra push-ups.

> # YOUR ATTITUDE TO EXERCISE COUNTS FOR AS MUCH AS THE EXERCISE ITSELF

You can't avoid exercise

My mother's generation, many of whom have lived healthily into their 80s and beyond, wouldn't have thought of exercising as an object in itself. They just kept healthy as part of normal life, and would go for a walk because they enjoyed it, not as part of a fitness regime. They weren't stupid – they knew it was also healthy to be active – but they'd never heard of bench presses or spinning classes or aerobics. Didn't need it. Which is a useful reminder that we don't need those things either. They're just a handy option for those who enjoy them and have the time and money.

When my mother was growing up, of course, it was much more common to walk or cycle to work, because fewer people had cars. Household chores took longer because there were no washing machines or vacuum cleaners or dishwashers or drip-dry clothes. And these things – along with walking or gardening or kicking a football around with friends – were plenty to keep everyone fit and healthy (so long as they didn't have other unhealthy habits). You might have done a 'keep fit' session of star jumps and lunges if you were in the army or at school, but most people just got on with their lives.

The same is still true now, except that most of us have opportunities to reduce the amount of physical activity we do. More people drive, and lots of us have household appliances to make life easier. We rarely need to go to the post office, or traipse to the bank, or even the shops, because we can do so much online.

We have far more leisure time than previous generations. That's why there's time to go to the gym, or out for a run. And yes, if we spend that time sitting in front of a computer instead, our activity levels will drop. But it's impossible, unless you're bedbound, to avoid exercise altogether. Just unloading the dishwasher or strapping a child into a car seat or walking up and down stairs is exercise. And that's all you need to stay fit – it's just a matter of quantity.

If you don't actually *need* to do enough of these activities to keep you properly fit, and many of us don't, you have options. One of these is to slob about and not be fit. OK it's not the recommended option, but it's still an option. If you don't want to do this (good for you) you can do the organised fitness, gym, running, cycling, classes thing – discrete chunks of time set aside for the purpose of being fit.

Then there's a third option, which is to live like my mother's generation. Keep busy, walk or cycle when you can even if you do have a car, and don't expect to sit down much until after your evening meal. No, you don't have to sell off your dishwasher and stop using your vacuum. But find useful activities – with the emphasis on 'active' – to fill your leisure time. Take the kids to the park and play catch with them instead of sitting on a bench looking at your phone while they play. Take up gardening or cricket, or even dressmaking or cooking. Go for walks – maybe get a dog if that makes it more fun. It's not that these things burn as many calories as running for an hour on a treadmill, but they keep you moving and stop you snacking and, what's more, they're productive and leave you feeling positive.

> ## DON'T EXPECT TO SIT DOWN MUCH UNTIL AFTER YOUR EVENING MEAL

Exercise isn't a dirty word

I'd hate to put together a group of Rules about exercise without acknowledging that some people just hate it. They don't enjoy doing it, it doesn't make them feel good afterwards, and every time they try a new habit it fizzles out because they have no motivation. These Rules are for you, and if you're one of these people you still need to stay healthy and to have a Rule that works for you. It's not realistic telling you that you should follow this or that regime, because it won't happen. You probably *want to* exercise, but you don't know how. It's alright, I get it.

It's recognised that some people have a more positive – or negative – attitude to exercise than others. There can be a genetic component in attitudes, along with environmental causes. People who are overweight are more likely to have negative views about exercising, whereas believing you have control over your own life (rather than everything being down to fate) increases the chances that your attitude to exercise will be positive.

If your thoughts about exercise are generally negative – you think it's difficult or too much effort or takes too long or is uncomfortable or embarrassing – you probably view with envy those people who find it fun and sociable and stress-relieving. So try to find other things to do which aren't exercise, and which you do consider fun or relaxing or sociable. Just make them active things which fit the bill, and don't define them as exercise if that's going to put you off.

For example, you could dance. Join a class or just go to clubs and discos. This isn't exercise remember (ugh, as if!) – this is fun. Or get a dog that needs exercising – the dog, not you, obviously. You're just there because it's fun hanging out with the dog and it needs a walk.

I use the punctuation point of getting to the end of each Rule that I write. I play a favourite song, and dance for three minutes, or however long the song I've chosen lasts. It's fun, and it marks a progress point in my working day (and it's a bit of activity after sitting at a desk).

If your issue is that you find traditional 'exercise' boring, find active things to do which never take more than three minutes. There are lots of good starting points for this – TV ad breaks, waiting for the kettle to boil, cleaning your teeth. These things are already boring, so adding a bit of activity into the mix isn't going to make it any worse, and actually it can help pass the time. If you like competing with yourself, see how many times you can run up and down the stairs before the kettle boils, or how many times you can touch the ceiling by jumping. Change the game if you start to get bored. I aim to get up and move every ad break – I might load the dishwasher, or put a laundry load in, or tidy something. If I'm watching so much TV that I've got through all those chores, I might see if I can play keepy-uppy without dropping the ball before the end of the ad break. So look for those two or three minute boring moments, and find something fun to fill them with that doesn't entail sitting down.

And if after all that you still want to work harder at being active without thinking you're 'exercising', walk faster.

THIS ISN'T EXERCISE REMEMBER (UGH, AS IF!) – THIS IS FUN

RULE 30

It's not about how you look

Here's something I've noticed again and again. I've known countless people who have taken up some form of exercise because they want to lose weight, or tone up their thighs, or get a six-pack. And some of them have succeeded in those aims. But here's the thing: they never seem to be satisfied. As soon as they've lost the intended amount of weight, they want to lose more, or they want to lose it in a different place, or improve their muscle tone, or get rid of their cellulite.

Being confident in how you look isn't about how you look, it's about how confident you are. If you're not happy about your size or shape now, you're not going to be happy about it once you've achieved your goal. Of course the exercise you get working towards it is probably very good for you, so I'm not knocking the activity. I'm just letting you know that once you've shed a few pounds you won't miraculously feel great about your appearance unless you were already feeling great about it before you started. OK you might get a short period of elation when you reach the target, but it won't be long before you start to wonder how you never realised that your shoulders are too narrow or your knees are too knobbly or your elbow skin looks a bit floppy.

If you don't feel confident about your appearance, fix the confidence bit, not the appearance bit. Because that's the thing that the rest follows from. I'm not saying that's an easy thing to do, but expending your effort in the right direction has got to be better than constantly trying to treat the symptom without ever addressing the underlying cause. Once you're happy in your own skin you can just exercise for fun and for the good of your health, and you'll feel great, with or without changes to the way you look.

You'll have read a few Rules about confidence already in this book,[10] so that's where to focus if you're not happy with how you look. Don't compare yourself negatively to others, either in terms of how you think you look, or in terms of how much exercise you think everyone else might be doing. You have no idea of their story, or what else they're doing when they're not at the gym (running marathons? Bingeing on chocolate?). If you want to look at other people, pick a role model or two who isn't in classic good shape but still looks fantastic and exudes confidence. It's a good reminder that you don't have to look like a model in order to feel like one. Listen to the narrative inside your head – do you tell yourself you're attractive, or do you criticise the way you look? When you look in the mirror do you think, 'Ugh, look at my hair. And my stomach. And my loose elbow skin ...' or do you think, 'Yeah, you look pretty good today!' That's not about how you look – it's about what you think. And that in turn will influence how you feel.

I can look in a mirror and choose to see all the good things (in my opinion, anyway) or all the bad things. Sometimes it amuses me to alternate these every few seconds and see how much difference it makes to how I feel, and how I think I look, despite the fact that literally nothing in the mirror changes. Try it. It will show you how important your internal narrative is to your confidence.

> # BEING CONFIDENT IN HOW YOU LOOK ISN'T ABOUT HOW YOU LOOK, IT'S ABOUT HOW CONFIDENT YOU ARE

---

[10] If you're reading it in order.

Habit is a good thing ...

Starting something new takes effort. Of course there's nothing wrong with effort, and it can be fun, especially if you're excited about the new something you're going to start. Sometimes effort or change can feel a bit daunting though, and that can be a barrier to becoming more active. It would be great to join a local badminton group, but will you get on with everyone there? Will they all be way better than you? Can you really afford it? Hmm ... actually this week is quite busy, so maybe think about starting it next week? That can go on for months, while you put off taking up any other exercise because you don't need it – you're about to start playing badminton regularly, after all.

You might be the kind of person who is forever starting new things, and relishes change. In that case the next couple of Rules might be more use to you than this one. However, many of us fall into the category of unconsciously resisting starting something new, of making excuses to ourselves to delay or avoid change.

If you currently sit at a desk all day and on a sofa all evening, and never take any exercise, it would be wise to make some changes. And it will help to recognise if making big changes is going to be more daunting, and to work with this rather than try to fight it.

For you, habit is your friend. The sooner you can embed exercise into your life as part of your routine, the better. So find things you can do which require only a small shift and which can become habitual very quickly. Once something is a habit, you barely notice you're doing it and it becomes easy to fit it into your everyday life.

Good exercise habits you can establish reasonably easily are things like walking up escalators instead of standing still, parking at the far end of the car park from the shops or station, meeting a friend for a walk instead of for a coffee. I have spent literally months of my life in the hallway waiting for kids to materialise and get into the car – now *there's* an opportunity to count how many times

I can touch my toes before the kids finally appear, or how many tracks I can dance to.

Once you're ready, you can move on to other habits such as going for a run or to the gym or joining that badminton group. But still recognise that *habit* is what will make it last. A badminton session on a day or time when you're often busy is going to take effort every time because if you only go every couple of weeks it won't actually be a habit. So unless you love it so much that your motivation is really strong, it's easier to pick an activity that is easy to stick to, and as frequent as possible. Fifteen minutes in the gym every weekday after work is more likely to happen than an hour once a week.

There's been a lot of research into how long it takes to establish a new habit, and the answers are slightly vague because it depends very much on the habit. It's bound to take longer to train yourself to do something long-winded and inconvenient, against something quick and simple that you barely noticed you weren't doing already. And faster to fix a daily habit than a weekly one. But generally speaking, you should find your new habit starts to feel natural within a month, and most habits will have become pretty well embedded after two or three months.

> FIND THINGS YOU CAN DO
> WHICH REQUIRE ONLY A SMALL
> SHIFT AND WHICH CAN BECOME
> HABITUAL VERY QUICKLY

... but you're in charge

For some people, there's an inherent risk with habits that you need to recognise. If you have a remotely obsessive or competitive nature, it can be quite hard to break habits. Now if all you're doing is jogging on the spot while you wait for the potatoes to come to the boil, you're probably fine. But you do need to make sure that you're running your life, and it isn't running you.

I know someone – and this isn't unusual – who decided that a wearable pedometer that counted his steps would be useful. He wasn't hugely fit but figured that 3,000 steps a day was a good starting point. Before long he was doing 5,000 a day, and then 10,000. Yes, 10,000 steps a day is great exercise, but if you *have* to do 10,000 steps a day, it can start to rule you. And that's not a good feeling. Certainly this friend of mine found he was fitting the rest of his life around completing his steps, and not breaking his streak. It may have made him slightly fitter, but it made him a lot less happy because it got in the way of other things he'd have liked to do.

Here's a question. Suppose there's a crisis at work and you're stuck at your desk until late. By the time you get home at 9.30pm you're shattered, and you've still only walked 2,000 steps. A neutral observer might say that it's an exceptional day, and you need to put your feet up just this once, rather than go out in the rain and walk round the block half a dozen times. A neutral observer might be right.

So what would you do? This is an example of where you find out who is in charge, you or your pedometer. Rationally speaking, your health and fitness aren't going to be affected in any calculable way if you settle for 2,000 steps just for once. So can you be rational? Whether your habit is steps, or a trip to the gym every Tuesday without fail, or never missing football practice – can you break the habit just occasionally when it makes sense? If not, then it's not you who's in charge. And while most of the time you and your pedometer (or whatever) get along nicely, it's important that when there's a disagreement, you assert your authority. Tell the activity tracker who's boss.

If you have the kind of personality that can fall prey to this – and lots of us do – just find ways to stop yourself falling into the more obvious traps. So maybe have a policy of randomly breaking the streak once every couple of weeks, just so it can't turn into a Thing. And be very wary of any exercise where you continually try to compete with yourself and build up to more steps, heavier weights, longer sessions. It's fine to start a new exercise gently and build up, but set yourself a level where you stop building and simply consolidate. And don't make yourself have to get there in an unnecessarily specific time frame. Being a slave to some self-imposed regime is miserable.

Before you ask – yes, I appreciate you can go too far the other way: letting yourself off the hook so often you barely ever exercise. If that happens, sounds to me like deep down you don't really enjoy that kind of activity, so maybe you should find an alternative that you don't want to excuse yourself from.

WHO IS IN CHARGE, YOU OR YOUR PEDOMETER?

Keep a lid on it

Just because something is good for you, doesn't mean that more of it is bound to be better for you. Yes, we should all be getting daily exercise. No, that doesn't mean the more exercise we do, the better. Look, food is good for us, but we know that too much food stops being good for us and can start going the other way. Why should exercise be any different?

I'm not a doctor, and I'm not going to tell you exactly how much exercise is too much for you – it depends on far too many factors. But it's likely to be counter-productive to do more than a couple of hours dedicated exercise a day, and most of us need far less. Of course it makes a difference how old you are, what exercise you're doing, and what you're doing with the rest of your life – do you do a desk job, or are you a lumberjack (or a professional athlete)? Do you spend all day running around after small children? What do you do with your spare time?

It's all too easy to get hooked on exercise for some of us.[11] The jury is out on whether it's technically an addiction, or a mental health disorder, but however you define it, it's not a healthy state of affairs and it won't make you happy. It's characterised by anxiety and can lead to any number of symptoms you don't want, from tiredness and mood swings to injury and loss of libido.

There are all kinds of reasons why people exercise too much, and often several of them apply. It can be associated with eating disorders, or it might be that your activity tracker causes you to feel under pressure to keep upping the ante. Maybe the endorphin rush you get when you exercise encourages you to keep working for more endorphin rewards, or perhaps the people around you all exercise hard and you're trying to keep up.

---

[11] I'm using the word 'us' here in its broadest possible sense.

Whatever the reason, exercising too much can be as unhealthy as exercising too little, especially when you take into account the stress, anxiety, depression and mood swings that so often go with it. So it makes sense to have a few ground rules in place that ensure you don't tip over into unhealthy levels of activity. You can pick the ground rules that work for you but, for example:

- Don't exercise if you're feeling unwell.

- Don't exercise if you're feeling very stressed or anxious (it can help with mild stress).

- Don't exercise for more than two hours maximum per day.

- Always leave at least six hours between exercise sessions.

- Skip one day every week.

- Don't exercise if you've had less than six hours sleep the night before.

That last one will vary from person to person, depending on your normal healthy sleep habits, but one of the effects of over-exercising is that it can mess with your sleep patterns. If you always take a break when you sleep badly, that's a good way to counteract this.

> **EXERCISING TOO MUCH CAN BE AS UNHEALTHY AS EXERCISING TOO LITTLE**

RELAXATION

We're concentrating on you in all 100 Rules in this book, and if you want to enjoy life there has to be space in it for relaxation. It's a busy world, and there will be extended periods when that's a commodity that's hard to come by. So it's important that you make the most of it.

Relaxation helps you recharge for the next onslaught of work, bills, commuting, kids, getting the shopping done, school, looking after parents, socialising, exercising and everything else that fills your day-to-day. It can be the reason you're able to keep enjoying those things (OK, maybe not the bills). The reason you can find the energy you need the rest of the time, rather than becoming increasingly anxious and fretful and unhappy.

So however busy your life is, you need to find ways of relaxing that allow you to stay happy – all else being equal – and to find the rest of your life manageable and enjoyable. In turn, that will help the people around you to enjoy their lives without either worrying about you, or finding you stressy and hard to be around. Yep, people who never relax aren't much fun in the long run, so you're doing everyone a favour if you can stay chilled, at least on a normal day.

RULE 34

Find your space

One of my children's very favourite places in all the world – his happy place – is standing just in front of Skógafoss waterfall in Iceland. Well, as close as you can get. If you're lucky enough to have been there you'll know that it's one of the most beautiful places on the planet. My son also loves it because the experience of standing up close is an assault on all your senses. The noise fills your ears, the waterfall occupies your entire field of vision, the spray dusts your skin – with the result that it drives out everything else. There's no room for stress or worry or anger. Consequently it's a consummately relaxing place to be. It's just a shame it's so far away and he's only ever had the opportunity to visit it twice. Still, other waterfalls are available.

I know a couple of people who achieve the same sense of immersion and absorption from gardening, which similarly occupies their mind and enables them to relax mentally, if not physically. For some people it's getting lost in a good book, or swimming, or painting, or yoga, or hanging out with small children. If you have something to do or somewhere to go that takes you away from the effort of everyday life, you're a long way towards being able to relax.

If you don't have a place or an activity that fills this role, it's a good idea to find one. Ideally it won't be in Iceland,[12] because it's important that you can get at it easily, on a daily basis, when you need to. It's often at the end of the day that you need to wind down, so find something that does the trick and be conscious of it, and of using it when you need to. 'I've had a tough day, I think I'll go and tinker with my train set for a bit.'

Indeed, it's worth having a selection of happy places for those days when you don't have time to nip over to Iceland. You might

---

[12] Unless you live there.

have a perfect outdoor spot you can get to at the weekends, but sometimes you need to wind down on a Tuesday. Or going for a run might be perfect for you, but it's not an option when you're on your own with small children.

We can't all have a 'relax' option 24 hours a day. Obviously you can't stand up in the middle of a difficult work meeting and announce you're just going fishing but you'll be back in a bit. However it's worth having something you can do at the end of each day which will help you unwind. Something you can dream about during your difficult meeting: 'When I get home I'm going to have a long soak in the bath.' That will help keep you going until your weekend fishing trip.

Look, we all do this stuff ad hoc from time to time, of course we do. But if you are conscious of when you need to relax, and you have a specific activity in mind that is achievable – or a choice for different scenarios – you're much more likely to use the prospect of it as a form of stress relief at moments of tension. And more likely to do the thing as soon as you get the opportunity later in the day.

IT'S IMPORTANT THAT YOU CAN GET AT IT EASILY, ON A DAILY BASIS, WHEN YOU NEED TO

Keep it quick

A fortnight's holiday can be a great way to relax, however it might be months before you get the chance. By then your stress could have reached the point where a fortnight barely cuts it. Stress accumulates easily, and the way to cope when things are tough is to have a pressure release that enables you to keep letting it go. Even if you can only release it in small quantities, this can make a big difference if you do it frequently enough. People who have strategies for relaxing in very short bursts find it much easier to keep their overall stress levels in check.

You need something you can do during a five-minute loo break at work, or when your children are screaming and you can't get out of earshot, or while your mother is out of the room. In fact, you want a repertoire of three or four different calming techniques, so there's a better chance of at least one of them being feasible.

Literally just counting to ten is better than nothing. Counting backwards from a hundred is better still – it requires just enough concentration that you can't focus on much else. If you get too good at it, start counting backwards in threes. Or do a simple breathing exercise – in through the nose and out through the mouth three times, or any other variation you come across that works for you. Half a dozen shoulder rolls, a quick sudoku if you have five minutes (that's another one that stops you thinking about anything else), a yoga stretch, YouTube cat videos, closing your eyes and visualising an Icelandic waterfall (or anywhere else that makes you happy).

The following do not count: tobacco, alcohol, chocolate, caffeine ... do your own relaxing, don't rely on substances of any kind to do it for you. At best they fool you into thinking things are OK, at worst you can become dependent on them during tough times. I'm not saying never indulge, just don't use them for stress relief.

Sometimes the source of stress is a colleague or someone in the family who really winds you up. In that case have an arrangement to text your partner or best friend with your latest whinge – or just write it down in an app on your phone. That can also turn it into an amusing anecdote, which helps to offset the frustration of it. Even just pulling a face at someone after they've left the room can make you feel better. Yes, obviously it's petty, but it still helps (just don't do it in front of an audience; we don't want everyone to know how petty you are).

These little moments of calm are pretty useful if you only have two or three minutes. Of course they won't always leave you feeling entirely happy without a care in the world. The aim is to drop the stress level, not eliminate it. Unless you're lucky, that will have to wait for when you're home later, or when the kids have gone to bed, or when this big exam or project or exhibition is over.

> ## LITTLE MOMENTS OF CALM ARE PRETTY USEFUL IF YOU ONLY HAVE FIVE MINUTES

Train your mind to relax

The human mind is an extraordinary thing. The more you use and reinforce those neural pathways, the stronger they get. In the same way you've learnt to salivate when you see or smell food, so you can train your mind to relax in response to certain things.

So if you routinely relax your mind by closing your eyes and taking deep breaths, or by playing patience, or by going for a five-minute walk, your mind will learn to relax when it receives these triggers. Once you've trained your mind to associate these ploys with relaxing, it will get the message and drop into relaxation mode pretty quickly as soon as you start.

If you think about it, it will be much easier for your mind to relax in response to these activities if it's not very stressed to begin with. No, bear with me, that's not as stupid as it sounds. Clearly strategies that only reduce your stress when you're not feeling stressed in the first place are of questionable use. But think about it: if you're training your body to run a marathon, you start by running just a few kilometres and then build up. In the same way, if you train your mind to relax when it's easy, it will start learning to associate those same actions with relaxation even when you are under pressure.

So don't gloss over this Rule on the grounds that you're not stressed at the moment. Good! Perfect timing! Now is exactly the moment when you should be establishing these techniques so that they really work when you next need them. And it's only a matter of time – sadly all our lives go through stressful episodes, sometimes for a prolonged period. Whether a member of your family is seriously ill, or your job is on the line, or your relationship is falling apart, or you can't make your mortgage repayments, there will come a period of weeks or months, maybe more, when everything you can do to keep your anxiety or fear in check will be precious.

Of course when that time comes it will be great if you can spend as much time relaxing as possible. Holidays or open-air trips or evenings with friends or trips to the gym, they'll all play a part. However, those frequent little moments throughout the day will keep pegging back the stress to a manageable level, and keep you going between the more dedicated periods of relaxation. But only if your mind is trained for it, and can shortcut straight to relaxation mode almost the moment you start.

This is also useful if you need to relax quickly just ahead of some activity. For example if you regularly compete in some kind of sport and get anxious just beforehand, or maybe find it nerve-racking giving a presentation and want a quick technique you can use immediately before you start. Those are the moments when there isn't time to take a few minutes to get into the mood. You want your mind to relax automatically as soon as it gets the signal.

> **ALL THOSE LITTLE MOMENTS OF RELAXATION THROUGHOUT THE DAY WILL KEEP PEGGING BACK THE STRESS TO A MANAGEABLE LEVEL**

Plan your breaks

When I was 18, I had two good friends who decided to take a gap year between school and uni to go travelling. They were going to spend about eight months working, and then the last four months on an extended interrailing trip around Europe. They planned to visit just about every country, and spent months researching the best route to take, where they could stay, the sights they mustn't miss and so on. They spent hours together every week planning their big trip and talking to everyone about how exciting it was going to be. And then suddenly, about a month before they were due to leave, they called the whole thing off. The rest of us all asked why, of course, and they explained that they'd had such a fantastic time planning the holiday that they knew the real thing just couldn't live up to their expectations.

I can recall a particularly tough period of my own life when I used, about twice a year, to get a weekend off when I could go somewhere secluded for one night and just stop for a bit. The only trouble was that by the time I'd been back home for 24 hours the relaxing effect had completely worn off, and I started to wonder why I bothered. Eventually a couple of weekends fell through at the last minute and I gave up trying. And that's when I realised just how beneficial the weekend breaks were, but not in the way I thought. The benefit was almost entirely before the event. True, the relaxing effect wore off fast, but I hadn't taken into account the massive benefits of anticipating the weekends.

You don't need a Rule to tell you that having a holiday can be relaxing. I imagine you've worked that out for yourself. But don't underrate the importance of looking forward to it. Appreciate it, savour it, enjoy it while you're waiting for the holiday to start. This ekes out the relaxing effect much better if you're conscious of it, and it helps to avoid disappointment. The more we need a holiday, the more devastated we can feel if it doesn't live up to expectation. If you've got every last inch of pleasure out of the expectation, and you know you have, it's far easier to feel the benefit regardless of what happens when the holiday finally comes around. Thinking about relaxing on a beach, or snuggling up in front of a log fire, or gazing at the view from half way up a mountain is doubly relaxing when it's about to be real. So suck all the relaxing value from that and, whatever happens, they can't take that away from you.

Some people already enjoy planning everything down to the last detail and researching all the things they could do while they're away. Some of us like surprises and prefer to leave it all to chance and spontaneity. If you're a 'don't overplan it' kind of a person, it doesn't mean you can't still enjoy the anticipation fully. You'll just enjoy it in a different way, with less itinerary-writing and more visualisation. Imagining the things you *might* do is just as much fun for you as writing lists of tourist sights is for someone else. So no excuses if you don't make sure you get your money's worth from the holiday even if it gets cancelled at the last minute.

> ## APPRECIATE IT, SAVOUR IT, ENJOY IT WHILE YOU'RE WAITING FOR THE HOLIDAY TO START

RULE 38

You won't relax if you don't try

Some people – and you'll know if this is you – seem to need a Rule about holidays not actually being relaxing if you don't let them. If you insist on dealing with all your emails as they come in, even if you're on the beach or at a meal out with your family, you have no one to blame if you don't feel relaxed at the end of the holiday. Your family on the other hand know exactly who to blame, because this actually ruins their holiday too. Why are you doing it to them?

If you holiday alone, I suppose this kind of behaviour is your choice. But a word in your ear: you're wasting your money going on holiday if you don't allow yourself to relax and enjoy it. If you holiday with other people, this is simply unacceptable. The only excuse for it is that you might not have realised how miserable it is for the family and friends around you. But now I've explained it to you there are no excuses, so never do it again.

Very few people are as indispensable as they like to think when they're on holiday. So why do you do it? And don't tell me it's because your boss expects it – if they do it's only because you've trained them to expect it. Unless your contract specifically states that you agree never to take a holiday anywhere without 24-hour phone access,[13] you're allowed to go off radar. You can always claim to have been up a mountain, or scuba diving, or on a submarine or something. Sure, if there's a crisis your boss might possibly want to check in with you briefly, but we're talking the kind of thing that happens once every dozen holidays, not constantly on every holiday – even if you are the boss. Make sure you plan properly for not being available, delegating responsibilities in your absence and scheduling things to fit round your holiday,

---

[13] And I'd suggest you don't sign that contract.

and there's no need to be at the end of a phone or email. If you were in hospital your office would manage without you, so let them manage when you're away – it's much easier because it's planned and expected.

Think about why you like to stay connected when you're on holiday. And be honest with yourself, because there'll be a reason. A deep down reason. Does it make you feel important? Are you scared of what might happen if the office discovers it can manage fine without you? Do you like to feel needed? Have you forgotten who you are when you're not working? None of these is a good reason to ruin the holidays of the people you're with. But they are feelings that it would be wise to analyse and get to the bottom of. Holidays are normal and just because the department ticks over for a week or two in your absence – because you planned it well – doesn't mean your boss is going to wonder whether they even need you. If you don't get to the bottom of your need to work through your holidays, you're never going to be able to relax and enjoy a break.

So if you must check in, switch your phone on once at the end of the day, and leave it at that. Don't reply to anything that you don't absolutely have to. Set auto-replies so people know they can't contact you. And if you still find it a struggle to separate yourself from work, take holidays in Antarctica, or the Amazon, or underwater, or somewhere no one can expect you to get a phone signal. Or at least tell the boss that's what you're doing.

> **IF YOU MUST CHECK IN,
> SWITCH YOUR PHONE ON
> ONCE AT THE END OF THE DAY**

Live in the present

Much of what makes us feel stressed or anxious is about the future: how will this meeting go, what if that happens, suppose I fail at this? Up to a point this is useful because it enables us to plan and take precautions and anticipate pitfalls so we can avoid them. However, there's no getting away from the fact that it can be stressful.

Another bunch of worries relates to the past: should I have made a different decision, why did this happen, what do I wish hadn't changed? This can help us avoid repeating mistakes, even though it sometimes makes us feel regretful, guilty, frustrated or worried. It's impossible never to live in the future and the past, and indeed it's a useful thing to do a lot of the time, and arguably part of what makes us human.

Nevertheless, both the past and the future can be beset with anxieties. The right happy memory or joyful anticipation can be very relaxing, but most of us are inclined to start worrying sooner or later. So why not focus on the present? It's such a fleeting thing that it's much easier to find a little corner of it without worries. It's not an option 24 hours a day, but aim to find a few minutes every day when there are no immediate problems or worries. A few minutes when you can sit on a park bench, or go for a run, or settle with a cup of tea in your favourite chair.

That's a great start, and now you can take the process a step further. The idea here is to focus entirely on the present, and to take the role of an observer. Notice that there's a train passing in the distance, or that your hair is brushing the top of your ear, or that you can smell cooking. Narrow down your thoughts to only what is here and now. You can't help but relax because you're ignoring all the things that might make you feel tense.

I know, it's not quite so easy in practice. But like all things, practice is the key. Do this daily and you'll start to find it easier and easier – and we're back to training your mind to relax so it can drop into that mode readily whenever you need a few minutes' break.

You will find, especially to start with, that worries and anxieties creep into your mind when you do this. In the long term you'll be able to refocus on the present swiftly, but it will take you a while to get the hang of it. The trick is to remember that you're an observer, so you can watch your thoughts go by: 'Ah look, here's some stress about next week's presentation,' or 'Look at me worrying about my mum again.' The effect of this is to give you a sense of detachment from your fears and anxieties, so by keeping them at one remove, you're still able to benefit from the relaxation these few minutes are giving you.

> REMEMBER THAT YOU'RE AN OBSERVER, SO YOU CAN WATCH YOUR THOUGHTS GO BY

Relax holistically

We think of relaxing as being something that requires very little physical energy. And indeed that is one way to relax. However, it's worth considering which part of you really needs to rest. Having forty winks, or sitting in the sunshine, or doing some gentle yoga should certainly relax your body, but is that the part of you that needs it?

If you've been racing around and are worn out, or you've been on your feet all day, or you have an active and busy job, then you probably do need to relax your body. But suppose you've been at your desk all day, or on a series of frustrating phone calls to the phone company,[14] or writing a really challenging report. You may well feel the need to restore your equilibrium, but it's mental relaxation you need, not physical.

Or perhaps your emotions need a break, from a difficult colleague or a seriously ill parent or a demanding child. Physical rest can be a help, but it's a very indirect route to relaxing the part of you that really needs remedying.

So think about why you need to relax, and find something to do which really gets straight to the source of the tension. Personally, when I'm emotionally exhausted, my first choice is anything that makes me laugh. Yes, a brisk walk or a nap or a warm bath can all help, but laughter is the thing. That might be a favourite TV programme, or a phone call to one of the many people who can always make me laugh, or even turning my current source of stress into an amusing anecdote in my head, ready to make someone else laugh.

When I'm mentally overtired I'm more likely to turn to something that switches my brain off for a while, whether or not that means

---

[14] Can't imagine why that example came into my head. It's not as if I spent most of yesterday on the phone trying to get a phone line connected ... (oh, the irony).

physically relaxing. Playing patience on my tablet, reading a trashy novel, going for a run,[15] watching any kind of movie that doesn't require me to think. So yes, the hot soak in a bath, the yoga, the feet up with a cuppa, the nap – they're all in my repertoire, but I mostly use them for those days when I've been run off my feet.

If you want to get the most value from the time you have to relax, be conscious about why you feel the need for it. If you always think 'I'm exhausted, I need a nap' you'll get some benefit, sure, but you're missing the chance to relax better (if that's a thing). Of course there will be days when you're whacked on every level, in mind, body and spirit, in which case it's probably a good idea to throw everything you've got at it – within whatever time constraints you're under. It's still good to think it through and make sure you're doing your best by your drained emotions and tired mind, as well as your shattered body. Because those are the days you most need and deserve to relax in every way you can.

> # FIND SOMETHING TO DO WHICH REALLY GETS STRAIGHT TO THE SOURCE OF THE TENSION

---

[15] OK I'm lying about the run.

Get out of yourself

They say that a change is as good as a rest, and certainly having something that takes you out of yourself is a great way to switch off and unwind. Playing with a small child when you get home is a great antidote to a stressful day at the office, as is walking the dog or going to your local football team practice.

So if you're prone to stress, tension or anxiety, make sure you have a regular activity that helps you to switch off. Better still, more than one. You may already have plenty of hobbies and activities, but do they help you to relax? I have a friend who does lots of amateur dramatics. She loves it, but it brings its own stresses with it, from dealing with prima donnas to the pressure of learning lines. If she enjoys it of course she should carry on with it, but it isn't filling the role of a relaxing activity. She still needs to come up with an easy, fun, uncomplicated hobby or two for when she feels in need of a bit of TLC.

Think about your extra-curricular hobbies, and which ones truly help you to relax and unwind when life gets complicated. Look, you might as well be honest about it – these Rules are for you, and I can't help you if you don't help yourself. I'm not going to tell you to stop doing anything you love, so you're safe there. Although you might find that when you think about it, you start wondering why you still run the neighbourhood watch scheme, or go to Pilates classes, or knit, if it doesn't bring you any joy or relaxation.

If you realise they no longer make you feel good, drop them and make space for something that does. Don't tell yourself you'll be letting people down – there's always someone to take over, and you don't have to give immediate notice tomorrow. Extract yourself over a few weeks if that feels better. It's just silly to do something optional that you don't get anything out of any more, even if you once did.

But if you enjoy any of your current pastimes, carry on. Don't mind me. Anything that makes you happy is worthwhile. If it doesn't help you to relax beyond the effect of the enjoyment, you can find something new to balance it with which will help you unwind. So, what do you fancy?

You're looking for something you can do fairly often. For example, if you're a single parent stuck in a house with small kids, don't rely on an activity that requires you to organise childcare or it just won't happen often enough. Sure, sign up for it if it appeals, but have an alternative for those evenings when you have to be at home. And think about what kind of relaxation you really need (go back and re-read the last Rule if necessary).

Give serious thought to what will give you an outlet for tension or anxiety, but don't forget you can always abandon it and try something else if it doesn't give you what you need. We're all different, and what does the trick won't be the same for everyone. So don't let your friends pressure you into joining their salsa class, or making up a four at bridge, or becoming treasurer of the rotary club. This is for you, and only you can choose it.

> WE'RE ALL DIFFERENT, AND
> WHAT DOES THE TRICK WON'T
> BE THE SAME FOR EVERYONE

Get a good night's sleep

It's impossible to function well, and to feel relaxed, if you're not sleeping properly. We all have the odd night when we sleep badly – or brilliantly but not for long enough. But far too many of us get into habits we don't need to which mean that we regularly sleep poorly. And poor sleep over time can cause all kinds of problems, from grumpiness to diabetes and heart disease.

There's just loads of research into sleep, and it's stupid to ignore it. As well as more serious medical conditions, lack of sleep makes your brain foggy, makes you more prone to coughs and colds (good sleep helps your immune system), encourages you to put on weight by leaving you feeling hungrier, and can even reduce your libido. Which of those do you want to sign up for? Because that's what you're doing if you allow yourself to get into bad sleep habits.

And by the way, having a lie-in at the weekend might feel lovely, but it's not improving the outlook health-wise. You need to make sure you're getting the right amount of sleep routinely. I realise that there are some people who are genuinely struggling to sleep well despite following all the advice, but there are far more of us who moan we're not sleeping well when we're not actually giving sleep a chance.

This isn't a guide to sleep techniques, and there are plenty of good ones out there so I'll let you do your own research. You're a grown-up after all. What interests me is why so many of us allow ourselves to get into bad habits. And then do nothing about it but complain how tired we are. There should be a law that you're not allowed to complain or to be irritable unless you've genuinely been practising good sleep habits routinely for some time without success.

You see, for a lot of people, complaining about poor sleep is half the point. It brings attention and sympathy, or provides an excuse for functioning below par, or shows off how incredibly busy you must be – and if you're that busy, you must be really important, right? Or really put-upon and martyred, which also deserves sympathy. Sorry to sound harsh, but for the majority of people – not all – some variation on this is behind the complaints about sleep deprivation. And the failure to do anything about it.

Of course it's rarely conscious, or at least rarely thought through so calculatingly. However, even if it is drumming up a bit of sympathy or admiration, it's still not worth the downsides. This isn't a logical, intelligent, sensible way to go. You'd feel so much happier without the moral support but with a good night's sleep.

So read the guides to better sleep, and follow their advice. Or if you insist on cramming too much into every evening, staying on your phone until late at night, avoiding routines that your body clock can keep up with, and otherwise ignoring all advice, at least don't come whingeing to the rest of us about it.

> YOU'D FEEL SO MUCH HAPPIER
> WITHOUT THE MORAL SUPPORT
> BUT WITH A GOOD NIGHT'S
> SLEEP

Love the sunshine

Earlier generations were great believers in 'fresh air' and it's become rather lost over time. Plenty of people nowadays barely go outside unless they have a free day when the sun is shining. But fresh air does so much more for you than simply make you feel good at the time. You don't need to read this Rule if you're a farmer or a tree surgeon, or if you regularly spend all your free time gardening, but most of us would do well to get more fresh air than we do.

I'm lucky – I live in the countryside. However even if you live in the city, where the air is less clean, it's almost certainly better for you than the air inside your office or workplace, so long as you avoid busy traffic. And if you can get out of town at a weekend or in the evening, it's even healthier. Literally just being in the great outdoors is a boost, even if you do nothing when you get there. Of course exercising is even better, whether it's a gentle stroll or a strenuous cycle ride, and it gets even more of that lovely oxygen into your lungs. If you have a garden or a yard it's a better space for any kind of stationary exercise than indoors, so get out there to do your press-ups or dancing or weight training.

This isn't just me and a random old-fashioned idea of what makes you healthy. This is backed up by loads of research into all the various ways that being in the fresh air will make you feel good. So if you want to look after yourself well, build time outside into your regular schedule, and don't just save it for sunny days.

Just a few minutes of fresh air each day will help improve your sleep (so no more moaning about another bad night), bolster your immune system, and boost your energy. It increases your oxygen levels which will increase the amount of serotonin in your system – that's the hormone that helps you feel happy and relaxed. Research shows that if you're breathing in the scents of plants and flowers and the natural world, that will boost serotonin levels too. You could just buy yourself some flowers from the florist on the way home, but far better to spend some time in a wood or a garden or on a beach or in the park.

And then there's vitamin D. Your body makes this from the UVB rays in sunlight, and it's good for your bones and your teeth and your immune system, among other things. You have to go outside for it because the UVB rays can't travel through glass, so sitting next to the window doesn't cut it. Here in the UK you should be able to make all the vitamin D you need from the sun for about six months of the year, but only if you spend several minutes a day outside. The rest of the year you can get it from eating eggs and oily fish and red meat, but don't let that stop you going outside for all the other benefits it gives you.

They say there's no such thing as bad weather, there's just the wrong clothes. All the benefits of being outdoors apply when it's cloudy, raining, snowing or blowing a gale. So there's no need to be a fair-weather outdoors type. Go on, put on your scarf and gloves and get out there. It's what people who live in the frozen North do all the time, and it's great – so long as you're dressed for it.

> LITERALLY JUST BEING IN THE GREAT OUTDOORS IS A BOOST, EVEN IF YOU DO NOTHING WHEN YOU GET THERE

Zen it

Here's a lesson I learnt like a thunderbolt from someone else, and it came as a huge surprise after decades of being intermittently stressed and frustrated about various and random things, as most of us are. Well it may surprise you to know that most of that stress is optional. There's simply no need for it. You can just turn it off.

Yeah, me too. I didn't believe it at first. All those years of getting stressed by slow traffic, and difficult colleagues, and exams and interviews, and computer malfunctions, and the hot water running out just as I got under the shower. All wasted. I didn't need to get stressy about any of it. I just wish someone had explained that to me sooner.

It wouldn't be putting it too strongly to say that it's changed my life. I've become calmer than ever before, and that adds to my enjoyment of every single day. And all because someone told me that I didn't have to get stressed – it was a choice I was making and I could stop making it.

That was the epiphany – the realisation that I was choosing it, albeit entirely unconsciously. If the traffic is slow, it's slow. Nothing I can do about it. But here's a choice I do have: be stuck in slow traffic feeling stressed, or be stuck in slow traffic feeling calm. No prizes for guessing which of those is preferable.

When we feel stressed by these everyday irritations, we have an internal conversation about how irritating it is, and how we'll be late, and how we already have too much to do, and how this will throw the whole day out ... but none of those escalating, frustrated thoughts will speed the traffic up. So why think them? Just dump it. Turn up the radio, sing along, and think about something else.

The language around stress and frustration isn't helpful, and is a lot of why it never dawns on us that we have a choice. We say, 'the traffic stressed me out' or 'my colleague is driving me mad' as though *they* have the control and they're visiting the frustration upon us. It makes us victims. And no one ever explains that actually we *chose* to be frustrated by the traffic, or we *let* our colleague drive us mad. And if no one tells you that, why would you ever stop feeling stressed by these things?

I appreciate that for people with real anxiety issues this Rule isn't going to turn everything around in a moment. And indeed if you aren't hugely anxious but for some reason you want to continue getting stressed, you carry on. It's no one's problem but yours, and if you don't see it as a problem that's great. I'm just trying to help if, like me, you've spent a lifetime feeling intermittently stressed and would quite like to stop now.

Since I learnt this Rule I've successfully applied it to everything from a car break-down to moving house – yes it even works for big stuff. The only thing I haven't managed to apply it to is those rare occasions when I'm seriously anxious about someone I love – not minor concerns (it still works for those), but real long-term health worries. There's too much deep emotion there and, while the zen approach still eases the stress, it's impossible not to care.

NONE OF THOSE ESCALATING, FRUSTRATED THOUGHTS WILL SPEED THE TRAFFIC UP. SO WHY THINK THEM?

FOOD

For such a basic essential of life as food, we don't half find it tricky to manage, especially in the Western world where there's generally choice and ample supply. It's one of the foundations of life, but you don't hear people saying 'I have real issues with water', or 'I just find it really difficult to breathe the right amount of air'. Nope, food has a special place for us, and becomes deeply intertwined with our psyche so that what we eat becomes a reflection of how we feel, how we grew up, how we view ourselves.

Part of the problem of course is that food can taste really good. It's hard not to enjoy a slice of hot buttered toast on a chilly afternoon, whereas we don't really notice the air we breathe. So then maybe we want more toast, or perhaps something to go with it ... I've never been tempted to breathe more air than I need, but I've often been tempted to eat more food than I need.

And of course too much food can be unhealthy. So can too little food. Or just the 'wrong' food. Our relationship with it is complex and for many people it feels problematic and interferes with enjoying life and staying healthy. If you struggle with food at times, it's important to understand some of the Rules around it in order to make sure its place in your life is a positive one, that makes you happy and keeps you healthy.

RULE 45

You really are what you eat

First of all, let's just establish why it matters that you get to grips with food. What you eat makes a huge contribution to your physical health, and there's now plenty of science to show it also affects your mood. Yep, the right eating habits will actually make you happier.

This isn't a healthy eating guide. There are plenty of good ones around, and the gist of them all is the same. Eat a balanced diet of mostly natural, unprocessed foods, with lots of fruit and vegetables, some protein, some starch, not too much of anything, Bob's your uncle. I know this observation will be wasted on the young, but as you get older and more at risk of heart disease, diabetes, high blood pressure and all the rest, the more you wish you'd got into good eating habits earlier.

The hard evidence for the link between food and your mood is much more recent, and a growing number of studies show that eating well really does improve your mental health, reduce depression, and give you energy. I'm not talking about that bar of chocolate that makes you feel good for five minutes. And this isn't about special foods or magic ingredients or fancy diets. It's just about eating the things we've always known were good for us (as outlined above), alongside *not* eating the things we've always known were bad for us: processed foods, things cooked in lots of oil, fizzy drinks, sugary stuff ... oh, you know what they are.

It also helps to eat regularly. If your blood sugar drops you're more likely to feel tired, depressed or 'hangry', one of the most well-known correlations between your mood and what you eat. And stay hydrated. It doesn't have to be water – although water is ideal – just non-sugary drinks.

There are lots of ways of doing this, not a single 'right' way. You can go for a Mediterranean diet, or a Japanese one. You can be vegetarian, vegan, or not, although research shows that too much red meat can increase depression and anxiety. So can too little, actually, although if your mental health is good on a vegan or veggie diet, why worry? If it isn't, you might want to reconsider, or make double sure you're getting all the relevant nutrients else-where. When it comes to looking after yourself, and being as happy, healthy and energised as possible, don't let other people tell you what you should or shouldn't eat. Except me, obviously. I'm telling you to eat whatever works for you – just take it from the long list of stuff that's good, and mostly avoid the stuff that isn't. Not complicated.

By the way, if you think this is obvious (and you'd be right), con-gratulations. It's reckoned that about 90 per cent of people eat an inadequate diet, so if this Rule is a waste of time for you, that puts you in the top 10 per cent. Well done.

> # THERE ARE LOTS OF WAYS OF DOING THIS, NOT A SINGLE 'RIGHT' WAY

Don't get picky

I know a couple who set up an eco-lodge on the beautiful West Indian island of Dominica, which is relatively untouched and where the indigenous Carib people still live in the way they have for centuries. One of the locals used to help out in the kitchen. Apparently when the owner was cooking she would invite the Carib woman to taste the food and ask her opinion. The woman was happy to taste it but had no way to say whether it was good or not. Her reply was, 'It's just food, and I'm grateful to have it.'

I've never forgotten this, and the sudden awareness it gave me of how much we take food for granted in most parts of the world, and particularly the West. We think nothing of saying, 'I don't eat this' or 'That makes me feel bloated' or 'I never touch cheese after 6pm.' What happened to just being glad not to go hungry?

I'm not saying that we shouldn't have preferences if we're lucky enough to be able to, but we should recognise that food fads are actually a luxury that many people can't afford and would have no concept of. I'm not talking about serious nut allergies and the like, but about intolerances or preferences or, in some cases, just plain pickiness. Personally I really don't like very bitter salad leaves, and continue to leave them on the side of my plate if I'm given them, but I try to remember that it's a luxury to do that, and in a different life I'd be grateful for them.

Veganism and vegetarianism for example are a luxury, for people with a first world lifestyle. They may be excellent diets – for you and the planet – and you should be free to make that choice, but don't lose sight of the advantage you have in being able to make it. This is about perspective. Make whatever choices you are able to, but recognise that for many people the world doesn't fall apart if they have to eat bread that contains gluten. Indeed it may be the thing that holds their world together.

And actually, the people I know who seem to have the easiest, happiest, healthiest diets are the ones who keep it simple. There might be the odd foodstuff they wouldn't choose to buy for themselves, but they'll eat pretty much anything without fuss. The danger of pickiness and fads is that they become a displacement, or an excuse, for the things you're not happy with in yourself. They can encourage you to focus on your own problems, to look inwards, to make it all about you. And that never makes you happy. Much better just to get on with life and eat what you're given (like I had to as a child).

I'm aware I may be upsetting some people here. But you've bought this book to learn what works, not to hear your own opinions reinforced. I'm sorry if it's uncomfortable, but focusing too much on yourself is going to make you less happy, not more so (see Rule 1). And that's not what either of us wants. So avoid the odd food you really don't like, or don't believe in, or doesn't agree with you, but don't talk about it – it's your stuff, and no one else needs to know – and don't let it become a Thing.

> THE DANGER OF PICKINESS AND
> FADS IS THAT THEY BECOME
> A DISPLACEMENT

RULE 47

Nurture your relationship

I've known several people who have gone on eating regimes of some kind where they avoid regular food altogether. Maybe they switch to some kind of astronaut-style powdered food formulated to provide all the essential ingredients. Or they go on a crash diet where they consume only shakes. And the thing I've observed almost every one of them struggle with is the principle of cutting off diplomatic relations with 'normal' food.

We all have a close, lifelong relationship with food, whether it's healthy or unhealthy. And trying to sever the relationship completely is incredibly difficult. The people who do best on these food-free regimes are almost always the ones who retain a relationship with food – even if they're not actually eating it. For example parents who continue to cook for their children despite not sharing the food themselves. It interests me because it highlights the importance we all place on that relationship.

If you're not entirely happy with your own eating habits – you feel you eat too much, or too little, or the wrong things, or at the wrong times – it reflects the fact that you're not happy with the relationship. And, as with all relationships, that means working through how to put it back on course. We're all born with a perfectly good relationship with our food. We feed when we're hungry and not when we aren't. At some stage, often earlier than we can remember, the relationship begins to grow and develop and become more complex. This is generally a response to our environment: whether food is hard to come by, whether too much unhealthy but delicious food is on offer, how our parents behave around food, how they expect us to behave.

For some of us, all these factors build into an unhealthy relationship. Lots of complex and perhaps conflicting undercurrents build up to the point where it's no longer as simple as eating something healthy when we feel hungry. The relationship starts to dominate, to occupy more of our thoughts and our lives than is good for us.

It isn't in our own interests to over-complicate our relationship with food. We renew the acquaintance several times a day, and the simpler it is, the easier it is to keep it healthy. To keep ourselves healthy.

Of course once you have a dysfunctional relationship with food, it's not easy to put it right, just like any relationship. The first step, however, is to recognise that the relationship is the root of the problem, not the fact that you eat when you're anxious, or can't wind down without a glass of wine, or can't stop at just one biscuit, or get shouty if your meal is delayed. Those are just symptoms.

So that's where to focus your efforts. Don't keep fighting to leave the rest of the biscuits uneaten. Concentrate on the relationship, and the rest of it will eventually take care of itself. I appreciate that for some people this can be a lifelong challenge, and serious eating disorders often demand professional help with it. However the aim is the simple, uncomplicated relationship with food that you had as a baby.

> # WE'RE ALL BORN WITH A PERFECTLY GOOD RELATIONSHIP WITH OUR FOOD

Understand your issues

When couples argue about who should do the washing up, it's not generally about whose turn it is. It's about some underlying issue such as one of the two feeling taken for granted. Most relationship fights are like this – something has triggered a deep-seated gripe, and the argument is focused on the something (the washing up) rather than the real problem (feeling exploited).

The same thing happens in your relationship with food. When you eat through a packet of biscuits it's not actually about being hungry. It's about something far deeper. The underlying reason varies – comfort, boredom, reinforcing low self-esteem – I can't tell you exactly what it is in your case. You'll have to work that out for yourself. Until you do, you'll struggle to stop eating biscuits.

I'm often frustrated when I read about studies into obesity that seem to assume that people who eat more than is healthy are doing so because they feel hungry. They focus on how to help people recognise when they feel full, or understand that it's fine to feel hungry before a meal. While I'm sure this has its place, for millions of people overeating has nothing to do with feelings of hunger. Feelings, certainly. But different and far more complex ones.

Sometimes our issues are pretty straightforward. Some people eat biscuits because they've given up smoking and it gives them something to do with their hands. If it's causing problems it needs addressing, but it should be fairly straightforward to fix. However sometimes the issues are much deeper, and maybe stretch back into childhood. They may be born of some trauma, or a dysfunctional attitude to food within the family when you were a child.

We all have issues of one kind or another. They don't play out in our attitude to food for everyone, but for a lot of us they do. My generation grew up after the war with mixed messages. Our parents had lived through food shortages and rationing and taught us to eat everything that was put in front of us. Only by the time we were teenagers we could get whatever we wanted, so a lot of us ate it all and struggled to keep our weight healthy. This was no one's fault, but it did leave plenty of people with an issue about being programmed to eat everything and then having to *not* eat everything.

In order to deal with this example, you have to understand that you have an underlying and deep reluctance to leave any food on your plate. This is not because you're hungry, or have a problem with 'waste' (ooh, I heard that word in my mother's voice). It's because you were unintentionally brainwashed as a child, and you have to reprogramme yourself. If you can do that, you're in with a chance of cutting down your food intake. If you don't recognise and address it, you'll never solve the problem.

WHEN YOU EAT THROUGH
A PACKET OF BISCUITS
IT'S NOT ACTUALLY ABOUT
BEING HUNGRY

RULE 49

Beware food rules

Some people are unfortunate enough to have very complex and unhealthy issues in their relationship with food. Many of us have some underlying beliefs or attitudes that colour the relationship, and which it helps to recognise. So here are a few of the more common and unhelpful patterns we can get into as a result of the way we relate to food.

I've already touched on the first, which is the inability to leave food on your plate. You don't have to have grown up in the 1950s and 60s, or in the West, to have been taught from an early age that you must finish everything on your plate. At school we were never allowed to leave the table until every last morsel was eaten. My headmistress when I was about five would say, 'Don't leave anything on your plate. Think of all the starving children.' I could never understand at that age how they would be helped by me clearing my plate. Surely it would be better to leave something and they could have it?[16]

It's interesting how the human mind works. There were lots of other rules when I was young which would serve most of us very well now, and which somehow failed to embed themselves into my psyche: never eat between meals, never eat in the street (or in the car), it's good to feel hungry before a meal. From observation I'm not the only person whose mind glossed over these less welcome rules.

Here's another childhood admonishment you may have heard: 'You can't have pudding unless you finish your main course.' This translates broadly in your subconscious as 'Sweet things are wonderful and you can't have them unless you work through the tedious savoury stuff first.' It's not actually healthy to grow up believing sweet foods are inherently much nicer than savoury foods, but that's what happens if you are raised by this rule.

---

[16] I do now understand that her point was about gratitude, not logistics.

Alongside this rule is the broader implication that all meals should be rounded off with something sweet. That can be a hard habit to break after you grow up – always wanting something sugary to follow. Incidentally, the only way I could find to avoid passing this on to my own children was not to give them any kind of pudding at all (except fruit) unless we had visitors.

Here's another common unhealthy rule, often perpetrated by primary schools as well as parents: sweet or unhealthy foods as a reward or compensation. For winning a race, or because you fell over and hurt your knee, or because you completed your homework or cleaned your room or walked the dog. Eighteen years of that, and you turn into an adult who tells themselves, 'I need chocolate, I've had a bad day,' or 'I deserve a treat, I worked hard at that presentation.' There's nothing wrong with eating the occasional unhealthy treat – the problem comes when you associate it with a particular behaviour. Much better for treats to be completely random, or perhaps associated with rare occurrences (holidays or Christmas or cinema trips) so they can't happen too often.

Oh, but not so rare they become deeply sought after. Tricky stuff this, eh?

> **THERE'S NOTHING WRONG WITH EATING THE OCCASIONAL UNHEALTHY TREAT – THE PROBLEM COMES WHEN YOU ASSOCIATE IT WITH A PARTICULAR BEHAVIOUR**

Don't diet

If you believe you weigh too much, and want to do something about it, the standard response is to go on a diet. Obviously. If you take in fewer calories, your body will have to burn its own and bingo! Your weight will drop. Duh. It's not rocket science.

There's no shortage of diets out there to choose from. They might not call themselves low-calorie diets. They might dress it up as high-protein, or low-fat, or intermittent fasting, or any one of a number of things, but the gist is always to take in less energy so you have to use up your own supplies. Some of them make a lot of sense, some are downright dangerous, and there are all points in between. It's a huge industry after all.

So here's my question. Why do so few people successfully lose weight *and keep it off*? If it's as simple as calories in/calories out, shouldn't there be far fewer serial dieters in the world? We all know that if you lose the weight and promptly revert to eating five chocolate bars a day, the weight's going to go back on. We're not stupid. And while a few people might fall into that trap, the vast majority are genuinely trying hard to keep the weight off. So what's happening?

I'm not a scientist, as you know, so I'm not going to attempt technical detail. However I do understand that, for example, genes play a big part, that for some reason men can generally lose weight more easily than women,[17] and that when you diet you retrain your whole metabolism. Suppose a healthy calorie intake for your height/activity level is 2,000 calories a day. You cut down to, say, 1,500 calories until you reach your target weight, and then start eating the recommended 2,000 a day to maintain that weight. Research is now suggesting that, counter to what you'd expect, the weight will go back on. Why? Because you've reset your

---

[17] How unfair is that?

metabolism to run on 1,500 calories a day, so what should have been the healthy intake – 2,000 – is now too much.

I imagine any scientist reading this will be cringing at the over-simplification of what is still a new area of research. However, I want to illustrate that losing weight is far more complex than just reducing your weight to where you want it, and then eating what is supposed to be right for that weight.

The key lesson from this is that it rarely works to go on a diet and then stop. If you want a permanent effect, you need to make permanent changes. Don't 'go on a diet'. Instead, make sustainable differences to what you consume, and be realistic about what you can maintain for life. Small incremental changes that you stick to might slow down the weight loss, but it's more likely to last. Start by just cutting out sugar in tea and coffee, or only having pudding if you're out or have guests (much more achievable than pretending you'll never eat another pudding as long as you live), or never shopping when you're hungry so you're less tempted by treats. Build these up slowly and manageably, and think long term but also long lasting.

> IF YOU WANT A PERMANENT
> EFFECT, YOU NEED TO MAKE
> PERMANENT CHANGES

Don't get hooked on sugar

I know – too late. At least for some of us. But listen, research is increasingly telling us that sugar is an addictive substance in a similar way to, for example, cocaine. That's because it has a similar effect on the brain, triggering the release of dopamine that gives you a kind of high. The more sugar you eat, the more your brain adjusts to it, so it wants you to eat ever more sugar to keep getting its reward of dopamine.[18] What's more, every time you reinforce that neural pathway, you establish your sugar-eating cravings more firmly.

I'm not pretending that you might as well take heroin as eat sugar. But it's useful to understand why you crave sugar – if you're one of the many people who does – in order to help you find a healthier approach. One where you're consciously in charge, and not the mere plaything of your brain chemistry.

By the way, for sciency reasons, refined sugars (that you buy in a packet marked 'sugar', or possibly 'honey' or 'maple syrup') are worse for you, and more addictive, than naturally occurring sugars such as those in fruit or milk. You may have noticed that you're more likely to crave chocolate biscuits than kiwi fruit, and that's why.

So if you want a healthy relationship with food, where you're not at the whim of urgent sugar cravings but simply eat when you're actually hungry, you'd do best to get your sugar from natural sources. There's nothing wrong with that. Sugar isn't bad in itself, so long as your intake is moderate, and you'll find that easier to achieve if you mostly stick to natural sugars. If you can

---

[18] Apologies once again to any real scientists out there for my oversimplification of sciency stuff.

eat one piece of cake a week and not crave any more, good luck to you (and please shut up about it and don't brag). If one piece always leads to three more – or the whole cake – it makes sense not to eat the first slice.

So you're already hooked, and you just want to stop eating so much sugar. In that case you need to devise an alternative strategy – or several to choose between – to discourage you from giving into cravings. Don't beat yourself up if this doesn't work every time from the off. You need to create fresh neural links to override the current ones, and that's bound to be hardest at the start. But persevere and it will get easier. Remember, you're not trying to beat the sugar itself, you're trying to control your brain's response to it.

The simplest strategy then, if you're actually hungry, is to eat a non-sugar-laden meal instead of a sweet snack. In any case it's wise to avoid getting too hungry between meals if hunger will prompt you to snack. If you don't need to eat, distract yourself – go for a walk, take a shower, phone a friend. Have several distractions ready in your mind so you'll be able to find one that works for you when you need it. And learn to recognise and avoid – where possible – obvious triggers such as tiredness and stress, and shopping when hungry.

> **YOU'RE NOT TRYING TO BEAT THE SUGAR, YOU'RE TRYING TO CONTROL YOUR BRAIN'S RESPONSE TO IT**

RULE 52

Food isn't wicked

When I was younger I had an aunt who, if you ever offered her a chocolate, would say, 'Ooh, I shouldn't really,' or 'Gosh, how naughty!' I used to think (but was too polite to say, of course) 'If you think you shouldn't, then just don't.' She usually did though. I don't really know why I'm singling out my aunt as this is a very common attitude – I suppose I noticed it as a child with her because I didn't understand it.

Listen, food – including sweet or fatty food – isn't good or bad or naughty. It's just food. There's no moral dimension. And if you start telling yourself you're being naughty or sinful or weak when you eat it, you're creating a whole new, and quite unnecessary, level of complication to your relationship with it.

It isn't naughty to eat unhealthy food. It's just unhealthy. And it's *your* health – you're not harming anyone else. You might prefer to avoid these foods, and if you decide to eat a chocolate or a dough-nut you might subsequently wish you hadn't. But it doesn't make you a bad person. There have been times in my life when I've regretted all sorts of things with hindsight – taking the bus instead of the train, mopping the kitchen floor just before someone spilt something across it, accidentally buying a book I already have.[19] But none of these mistakes have made me feel like a sinner. They're just things I've put down to experience and tried to learn from. So if you're offered a chocolate, either eat the damn thing or don't. But don't use it as an excuse to beat yourself up.

A lot of this is about the language we use, including the words we use inside our own heads. You don't have to say something aloud for the words to have an impact. And it doesn't matter how much you agree with all this rationally. If you still use words like 'naughty' and 'shouldn't' and 'temptation' and 'not allowed'

---

[19] Surprising how often I do this actually.

when you think about unhealthy foods, that's what you'll believe deep down.

So retrain yourself to see foods as morally neutral, along with your own attitude to them. It might be inadvisable to eat your way through a whole jar of cookies, especially if you do it routinely and your weight isn't healthy, but that's all it is. Just a decision that in hindsight you reckon you'll try not to repeat, for rational reasons.

By viewing your decisions about food from a rational rather than an emotional perspective, you'll find it much easier to untangle your knotty relationship with it. For some people this process can take years, but it will never happen if you don't recognise the issue and start to change your vocabulary and your inner dialogue around food.

IT ISN'T NAUGHTY TO EAT UNHEALTHY FOOD. IT'S JUST UNHEALTHY

It's not all about your weight

Some people, seeing a whole section about food in this book, might think it's all about your weight. Well it isn't. Rules about food are important even when your weight is healthy – indeed even if you *agree* your weight is healthy, which isn't always the same thing. You need to look after yourself around food regardless of your weight in order to be as healthy and full of energy as possible.

It's also a bad idea to choose what you eat simply on the basis of its effect on your weight. That can become an unhealthy focus in itself, and it could get in the way of that easy relationship you want with your food. You won't achieve that if you over-analyse it all the time. So keep things in perspective.

It's important for you to be as healthy as you can because that makes the rest of your life much easier to enjoy. And as long as your weight is broadly healthy, it's also important to stop sweating about it. For many people, stress about what they eat is actually not about maintaining a healthy weight, but about being confident and comfortable in their own skin – literally.

Worrying about your weight can become a displacement for worrying about your shape. If you lack body confidence, blaming your shape on your weight can be a lot easier than addressing the things you can't change (at least not without a lot of money and some painful surgery). So much simpler to tell yourself that everything would be fine if you could just shed a few more pounds, rather than acknowledge that it won't make any difference because that's not the real problem.

Listen to me. If you don't like your body now, no amount of weight loss, body building or even surgery is going to fix that. Because the problem is in your head, not in your body shape.

You must know plenty of people who don't have what the media like to portray as 'perfect' bodies and yet who are quite comfortable about it. From your own friends to actors and pop stars and disabled sports people. And that's down to attitude, not weight or diet.

No, I'm not saying it's easy. But at least address the right problem. If you're not happy with your body, fix the 'not happy' bit, and not the body. Learn to recognise that it's about the way you think, and not the way you look.

No one else is remotely as interested in your body as you are, and that includes your partner or potential future partners (if they really do care, they're not worth having). No one else has noticed that your bottom is a funny shape, or your knees are a bit knobbly, or you haven't got a six-pack. The world is full of people with funny bottoms and knobbly knees who still manage to have friends and lovers, so it can't actually matter, can it? So sort out your attitude, and stop fretting about your body.

> **IT'S ABOUT THE WAY YOU THINK, AND NOT THE WAY YOU LOOK**

RULE 54

Enjoy!

I know I've just given you several food Rules to think about and inwardly digest,[20] but I don't want you to keep thinking about them forever. Absorb them, integrate them, and then move on. I know it won't be quite that clean or simple, but it's really important not to obsess about food. If you have any issues with what you eat, how much you eat, when and where you eat, the worst thing you can do is overthink and over-analyse. Yes, you need to deal with the barriers to a healthy relationship with food. No, you don't want to take that so seriously that you think about food constantly.

As I mentioned before, the people who have the healthiest relationship with food, and are the healthiest generally, don't really sweat it too much (I'm excluding here professional athletes who have a strict regime when they're training). They mostly eat good stuff, when they're hungry, and have a few treats but not too many.

Moderation is crucial. If you decide you will *never* eat chocolate or sweets or cakes or puddings, you are almost certainly setting yourself up for a fall. And anyway, why shouldn't you eat them from time to time? If you feel well, and have a broadly healthy body weight, what's the problem? Even if you're overweight (I mean actually overweight, not just in your head) there's still no point setting yourself unachievable goals. We've already established that the only weight loss that works is a permanent – and sustainable – change to your eating habits. So you need to change to something you can live with for the rest of your life without being miserable. It may take you a while to reach your new way of eating (and that approach will work more successfully than changing overnight) but it's still asking for trouble if the final version involves never eating your favourite foods ever again. That's not going to happen.

---

[20] Sorry.

As soon as certain foods become verboten, you've made the relationship more complicated. If I say to you, 'Whatever you do, *don't* think about little white polar bears,' what's the first image that comes into your head? In the same way, if you tell yourself *never* eat chocolate, what are you going to keep wanting to eat?

Chocolate just isn't a problem so long as it's an occasional treat and you're not scoffing ten bars every day. So why deprive yourself permanently? Ditto any other food that you particularly like. Good food *is* enjoyable and there's no reason you shouldn't enjoy it. It's important that you're able to relax and eat what you like, in moderation where that's healthier, if you're going to have a chilled and easy relationship with your food.

> **IF YOU TELL YOURSELF *NEVER* EAT CHOCOLATE, WHAT ARE YOU GOING TO KEEP WANTING TO EAT?**

LEARNING

From the day you're born, learning is unavoidable. Some of it is instinctive, and some of it is foisted on you whether you like it or not. In amongst all the things other people expect or require you to learn, it's easy to lose sight of the sheer joy of learning something just for its own sake.

Mastering a skill – even just the basics – or starting to become an expert in a subject that fascinates you, will stimulate you, make you feel capable and good about yourself, and is a source of real pleasure. So it makes sense to feed your confidence and your enjoyment by aiming always to be learning something new.

Sometimes this happens without really trying. I can well remember learning to cook when I left home and discovered no one else was going to do it for me. And how fast I had to learn to be a parent when my first child was born. So it's not only about enrolling on courses or deciding to get a guitar. There will be times when life is throwing more than enough learning experiences at you for the moment. But there will also be periods when you're relatively settled in a routine you know, and that's your opportunity to pick up a paintbrush, or really get to grips with the history of railways, or join a reading group, or study for an online degree.

This time round, it's not about what other people think you ought to learn. It's about whatever takes your fancy.

Pick what you enjoy

Remember how miserable it was at school being made to study Maths, or History, or Needlework, or whatever it was you hated? It was so hard to make yourself focus, and the things you were supposed to be learning just took so long to absorb it was painful.

Well this time you're doing it for you, so you can wave a cheery goodbye to Geography or PE, and pick a subject you fancy. Yep, anything at all. You're welcome to go back and study Macbeth, or magnetism, or ox-bow lakes if you'd like to. But equally you can go for something obscure, non-academic, esoteric, unexpected – it's up to you now and *anything* goes.

The problem at school was that you weren't interested in literature or Latin or art, or at least not in the way it was being taught. You might have liked the idea of being good at it, but not the process of getting there. And not only did that mean you weren't enjoying the lessons, it also meant your brain wasn't disposed to learn.

I have a friend who really struggled with French at school. Gave it up in the end. Then a couple of years later her life took her to France and she found she wanted to learn the language after all. Within a very short time she was fluent. Same subject, but a different learning style and new-found motivation made all the difference.

So this time let's make sure you're in the best possible head space for learning. And the first and most important thing here is to enjoy the process. Not only will you learn faster and better that way but – and actually this is important – it wouldn't matter if you didn't. You're having fun. So what if your watercolour painting never gets good enough to make money from? Your time isn't wasted because you've learned more than you knew before, and you've enjoyed yourself. What more do you really need?

I know this might seem obvious to you, but I'm amazed at how many people choose to learn things that they don't really enjoy. The thing is – listen carefully now – that only *you* can decide what to learn. It doesn't matter if your dad thinks you should brush up your DIY skills, or your partner thinks you should learn Spanish, or your friends think you should go to salsa classes with them. This is about *you* learning what *you* want to learn, in the way you want to learn it – at a class, reading a book, doing an online course, just giving it a go mistakes and all – your topic, your style, your life.

If you agree that Spanish would be useful, or your boss wants you to gain another qualification, or now you've got a dog you have to learn to train it, well, that's all fine, but it's not you learning for yourself. You also need time to learn simply because you want to. And indeed you need to be free to stop if and when you find you're not enjoying it any more (might never happen, but it's an important principle).

> # IT'S UP TO YOU NOW AND
> # *ANYTHING* GOES

Find motivation

Following on from the last Rule, enjoyment is the biggest and most important motivation – you'll struggle without it. For some people, and some kinds of learning, that's all you need. Everything you learn motivates you to keep going and improve more or understand better. Suppose you've never really been much good at cooking and now you'd like to learn to do it well. You might find that your culinary successes keep you going in themselves, and every delicious new dish you cook encourages you on.

But suppose your cake doesn't rise, or your curry is bland, or your pudding doesn't set, or your pastry is soggy? The better motivated you are generally, the more likely you are to push through these disappointments and keep going until you can get them right every time. That's why you may need to find a motivation that carries you beyond the initial burst of idealistic enthusiasm. You know, the dream where you imagine yourself winning the London marathon, or having your paintings exhibited, or being offered a professorship.

For a lot of us, other people are what keep us going. Learning in a group, or being taught one-to-one by someone you respect, means there's someone else to bolster you if you become disheartened. If this works for you, it's worth exploring the options for learning alongside someone else. Indeed, for some people this is such a motivator that it might matter more to you than exactly what you're learning. And that's fine.

Some of us however would prefer to learn alone. Whether you're studying anthropology or learning the piano, you might want the freedom to do it when you please and at your own pace, and not have to perform in front of other people. Indeed if you're studying anthropology you might struggle to find anyone else keen to join you at any given time. So other people aren't always the answer to staying motivated.

One of the most practical things you can do is to set yourself realistic challenges. Build into your plans the expectation that you will progress slower at some times than others, and that you will make mistakes along the way. You're supposed to be having fun so don't push yourself so hard you forget to enjoy it. You might decide that by your partner's birthday in three months' time you'd like to be able to bake them a birthday cake. Plenty of room there for trial and error and laughing at your mistakes, but also an opportunity in three months to stand back and observe how much you've learnt.

Maybe you'd like to go on holiday abroad next summer, and be able to get by in the local lingo at least for basic interactions – buying a museum ticket, ordering a meal, asking directions. Look, this is for fun, so no need to demand too much of yourself. If you exceed your challenge that's lovely, but remember that life will get in the way of learning at times, and progress might be slower than you hope. What's important here is that you've built in moments to stop and look back at how far you've come.

> # FOR A LOT OF US, OTHER PEOPLE ARE WHAT KEEP US GOING

RULE 57

Decide what you want to show for it

Here's another possible source of motivation, or of demotivation if you don't get it right. When we learn things formally, there's usually some kind of qualification or certificate or letters before or after our name or some such official recognition of our achievement. For lots of us the prospect of this gives us a target to strive towards. Once we're clutching the certificate or the award we'll feel great, and the effort will all have been worthwhile.

Now I'm not knocking this in any way, and if it gives you a helpful incentive to learn it must be a good thing. But let's pick it apart a bit just so we know what we're dealing with.

Look, the whole education system trains us to believe that the point of learning is to come away with a qualification. We know that's not true though, don't we? The qualification can certainly help when we leave school, but the learning itself should be what matters. After all, passing a History exam doesn't actually mean that you now *know* history – I mean, there will still be some bits of history that you haven't learnt about. These certificates and grades are just random staging posts between total ignorance and absolute all-knowingness. Yes they may have some practical use, and you might find them motivating – which is great – but they are not an end in themselves. Except at school where they allow you to stop studying something you weren't enjoying.

The downside of this approach is that you can become fixated on reaching that milestone or qualification. It might matter when you're studying for school or work, but this learning we're talking about now is just for you, because you want to do it. If you fancy learning car mechanics for your own satisfaction, why does it matter if you have a certificate to say you've completed a course? What if you didn't feel the need to reach that level of competence?

What if you weren't interested in the theory stuff they cover, and just wanted to get your head under a car bonnet? What if you want to carry on learning – do you have to get all the way to the next level of qualification or not bother to embark on it?

There's no right or wrong answer here. You just need to make sure you've thought about it. Some people want a certificate to show they've run a marathon. Others just enjoy running and aren't interested in the distance they've covered. Maybe they *can* run 26 miles all at once, but they don't know and don't care.[21]

What matters to you? Do you want a qualification in Spanish, or do you just want to be able to converse when you visit the country? Will the prospect of an exam motivate you, or will it just constitute pressure that takes the fun out of learning? You're doing this for you, so do it however you like. Don't listen to anyone else, but do remember that you can change your mind as you go. It's not a fixed decision you can't alter. It's whatever you want it to be.

THE LEARNING ITSELF SHOULD
BE WHAT MATTERS

---

[21] Thank you, I'm aware a marathon is not exactly 26 miles. But I don't care.

Stay out of the ruts

The thing about learning new skills or acquiring knowledge is that variety is stimulating. You're exercising a new part of your mind, creating neural pathways, expanding your capabilities. So if you fall into a well-worn pattern, you just won't get as much benefit.

Suppose you learn to surf. Well done. You enjoy it so much you decide you'll learn kite-surfing next. Then wind-surfing ... Of course if you find you love these things it's great to keep going, keep learning new water sports. You're having fun and that's great.

However, don't imagine that when it comes to learning, you're expanding your mind as much as if you added something different into the mix, such as crochet. Don't panic, you don't have to learn to crochet if you don't want to – learning for yourself is all about doing what you want, remember – but don't fall into the trap of thinking that learning yet another water sport at this juncture will be the same as learning to knit, or to write computer code. Of course feel free to do it, but be aware that it would also be good to add a new kind of skill. It doesn't have to be today if you're busy, however don't tell yourself that you've ticked the 'learning new stuff box' just because you've now discovered a great parasailing course.

I know a couple of people who are serial evening class-takers. They move from one course to another, spending a few months or a year on each. If that's what they enjoy, it's not a problem. Generally the social aspect matters to them at least as much as the specific course, so they get pleasure from it on more than one level. However it's worth remembering that variety in learning isn't only about the subject matter, it's also about the method of learning.

You can spend years learning to play chess, or you can learn to make gravy in an evening. We've already established that you don't have to work towards some kind of qualification or contest of ability unless you want to, and that opens you up to being able to spend as much or as little time as you like. You don't have to become a cordon bleu chef. You might just want to put a bit of time into learning half a dozen useful vegan recipes. OK you'll struggle to learn some things in an afternoon, but remember that variety can mean five years spent learning a language, or half an evening reading up about type design. Vary the effort, the time, the style, and exercise both your mind and your body.

The aim is not to complete one kind of learning and then start a new one. Life's not like that. Some things you never stop learning, and others get boring or impossible to organise logistically. Sometimes you realise that you've tailed off without noticing, and there are other things you can only learn or practise at certain times (surfing is much easier to learn when you're by the coast, for example). So you're not aiming to learn a series of skills one after the other. You want to keep stretching yourself in a range of ways that weave in and out of one another, but make sure there's pretty much always something on the go.

> # YOU CAN SPEND YEARS LEARNING TO PLAY CHESS, OR YOU CAN LEARN TO MAKE GRAVY IN AN EVENING

Find your forte

We don't all learn in the same way, you know. When I was at school, teachers seemed to think that everyone learnt best by listening to someone drone on for hours, while simultaneously taking notes. They never taught us how to take notes effectively. They seemed to assume it was an innate skill.

People, in all their wonderful variety, have wondrously varied ways of learning. Teachers have a much better understanding of this than they used to – at least here in the UK – but there's always scope to push things further. Some of us find it easier to learn things by reading words, some by looking at diagrams, some by listening, or watching, or repeating by rote, or using mind maps or memory skills. If you're lucky, whoever is teaching you (at school, uni, work, evening class) will help you find your optimum learning style, but you have to take ultimate responsibility for understanding how your own mind works.

Everything and anything goes, and it's not your fault if information isn't coming at you in the best way. Many people with conditions such as dyslexia or dyspraxia can't listen and write simultaneously – something my teachers back in school never realised – and actually even the people who can do it will learn more effectively in other ways. Those dyslexic and dyspraxic students often excel, but only if they're allowed to learn in their own way.

I have encountered a huge range of ways of learning over the years, some of them very creative. The only thing that matters is that they work. One child I knew learnt his times tables by chanting them while marching up and down stairs – they just went in better than chanting them while standing still. I know someone who records all the key info before a big presentation by speaking it into her phone, and then plays it back to herself in her sleep the night before.

Another friend enjoys talking in different accents and will switch accents to learn a new topic because it helps to fix it in his mind. So at school in, say, Physics, he'd talk to himself in a Scottish accent while they were studying magnetism, Irish for electricity, German for the structure of the atom, Welsh for forces and gravity, and so on. He found it much easier to recall vocabulary and concepts if he had them separated out in this way. (I don't recommend this approach to learning languages, by the way.)

Speaking of which, some people learn languages better just by speaking them, others can't really make sense of them unless they understand the grammar. Some of us would rather learn to cook by following recipes carefully, others prefer to experiment. Otherwise known as making it up, but that's fine too.

So whether you're learning to windsurf or getting the lowdown on a new client, understand how your own mind ticks, and don't set yourself boundaries. The aim is to learn. If you've done that, your method must have been a good one, however left field it might look to someone else.

> ## YOU HAVE TO TAKE ULTIMATE RESPONSIBILITY FOR UNDERSTANDING HOW YOUR OWN MIND WORKS

RULE 60

Get your hands dirty

I know someone who is learning to play the bagpipes over Skype. Without any bagpipes. In fairness she's not doing it through choice, because it's hard to see how this can be as effective as learning with a real set of bagpipes under her arm. It's an extreme example of the principle that you learn most things better when you get actively involved.

This is most true of physical activities, but there aren't many branches of learning you can't apply it to. I was lucky enough to visit Italy as a child, and first-hand exposure to all those fabulous ruins brought Roman history to life when I studied it at school, and made it so much easier to learn and understand.

The more involved you are, the better you will learn. If what you really want is to hide in a corner with a fascinating book, and you don't care how fast or slow you learn, of course you're allowed to do that. But most of us find it more interesting, and more effective, to immerse ourselves when we learn.

It should be self-evident that if you want to learn a skill such as gardening or basketball – or arguably playing the bagpipes – you'll aim to spend plenty of time hands-on actually doing the thing. But maybe you're researching your family tree, or fascinated by string theory. Nevertheless, you can almost always find some way to bring these subjects to life[22] and deepen your connection by *doing* something rather than just sitting in front of a computer. I was hugely moved, on a trip to Amsterdam, by a visit to the synagogue where my grandfather's parents would have worshipped as children in the nineteenth century. That certainly made the family tree feel more real. Even as an amateur physicist you can seek out museums, talks and exhibitions to get you out of the house.

---

[22] Well, maybe not literally in the case of the family tree.

If you feel the urge to expand your mind but don't have a specific new area of expertise in mind – just a general feeling that you could do with fresh stimulation – look at options where you can *do* while you learn. A few years ago I became a school governor. I didn't know much about the education system but I thought it would be interesting to learn, and boy was I right. I learnt loads and found it fascinating.

School governing isn't for everyone, but you could volunteer at a local charity, or join the amateur dramatics society (there's always lighting or stage management if you don't fancy acting), or help run a local sports team, or join an orchestra or a band.[23] If you don't want to be sociable there are plenty of volunteers needed to do accounts or keep records or maintain websites or help organise behind the scenes.

You'll hardly notice how much you're learning in these roles until you take a step back and think about it, when you'll realise that you've been happily expanding your knowledge while stimulating your mind. And remember: this is for you, so if you find you don't enjoy it, or you love it for a while and then start to get bored, you can stop. You're a Rules player so I know you won't let anyone down. Organisations expect a bit of turnover in voluntary roles so just time it right and you'll be fine.

> ## THE MORE INVOLVED YOU ARE,
> ## THE BETTER YOU WILL LEARN

---

[23] They might require you to have an actual instrument, not an imaginary set of bagpipes.

RULE 61

Enjoy your mistakes

Mistakes are good. We like mistakes. We *love* mistakes. Mistakes are how we learn, how we improve next time. They make our neural pathways spark into finding a better solution. It's said that you can't ride properly until you've fallen off a horse at least three times. That's not because you're supposed to fall off the horse. No, falling off the horse is certainly a mistake. And you have to do it in order to learn.

I quite like cooking. I have even – very rarely – been known to cook puff pastry (I know, what's the point, you can buy it ready-rolled at the supermarket, don't know what I was thinking). Puff pastry is supposed to be tricky to cook, but it always worked for me. It rose light, fluffy and buttery every time. And that worried me, because I knew it was tricky, and I didn't really understand how I was getting it right. Eventually, after years of cooking it (albeit only about once a year) I took it out of the oven and it was heavy and soggy. At last! I *knew* it was tricky! I investigated where I'd gone wrong – turned out I'd let it get too warm before going in the oven, if you're interested – and finally I felt I understood how to cook it. No longer did I have to feel I was succeeding by fluke. I actually knew what I was doing. Funnily enough, that was the point when I started buying the ready-rolled stuff from the supermarket. Maybe I felt the challenge had evaporated. There was no satisfaction left in getting it right when I knew before I started that it would go fine.

Most schools don't encourage mistakes. Most bosses don't really like you to make them. They all know that we're supposed to learn from our mistakes, but really they'd rather we didn't make our mistakes on their time. But hang on ... you're in charge now. This is your learning, for you, and no one else cares about your mistakes. So you can make as many as you like. So what? Every mistake will show you where you need to focus if you want to improve, and that's really useful. And you can enjoy the fact that it's no one's business but yours.

Whether you're serious about gaining a qualification, or just trying your hand at a new skill to see how it goes, your mistakes will tell you whether you're pushing yourself too hard, not concentrating because it's too easy, finding one particular area tricky, better in the mornings, better around other people, can't focus when there's background noise, need to read up on a bit of info, should be more patient (that's one of my regulars) ... the more value you can get from your mistakes, the more you'll enjoy making them.

So relish your mistakes, embrace them, laugh at them. I can remember trying to hang wallpaper for the first time, with my sister – now that was a learning curve and no mistake. About the first half dozen attempts were genuinely laughable. In fact I can remember a lot of giggling about how badly we were doing. But I learnt loads (mostly that actually I really like my walls painted).

> # RELISH YOUR MISTAKES, EMBRACE THEM, LAUGH AT THEM

Don't slow down

When my elderly aunt was in hospital with a terminal illness, she had a Filipino nurse who she got on really well with. I remember visiting only a couple of weeks before my aunt died, and she was telling me all the fascinating things she'd learnt about the Philippines. If you're not learning, you're not living, and as far as my aunt was concerned she wasn't dead yet.

Learning isn't just about studying. It's anything that stimulates your brain in new ways – taking on a new job, getting to grips with the facts behind climate change, learning to play chess, starting your first vegetable garden. And if you never do any of these things, never do anything you haven't done before, then what's the point? Babies famously learn at huge speed, mastering everything from movement to speech to interpersonal skills in a matter of a few months or years. The rate of learning slows down only because there are fewer things you *have* to learn in order to survive once you get older. But the human brain is wired to keep learning indefinitely, so don't waste it.

Once you leave school, you start to learn about work, from commuting to budgeting, not to mention the industry you work in. If you have kids, you learn how to be a parent (or on a bad day, at least you learn how not to do it. We've all been there). There's plenty of knowledge and skills we pick up as we go through life, from politics to navigating an airport to breaking bad news to soft boiling the perfect egg.[24]

However, the more you learn in order to run your own life, the less you need to learn. There comes a time when you can get your eggs right every time, and you know the airport like the back of your hand. It can be tempting to sit back and vegetate. But actually, this is your time to do something really interesting to stimulate your

---

[24] Four and a half minutes.

brain, keep you young, give you something to get excited about. Whether you're 30 or 80, if the learning experiences aren't coming at you, get out and find them.

You can pick anything you like. How thrilling is that? Tracing your family tree, working on an environmental campaign, surfing, training to be a magistrate, embroidery, becoming a counsellor, studying Russian history. Just pick something – anything – that grabs you, and which you can fit into the jigsaw of your life. And don't stop there. Once you've got to grips with one skill, you can move on to another. You don't have to manically devote all your free time to learning, although that's fine. You might take on a fascinating voluntary role, or a new paid job, and do it for several years before you stop feeling you're learning. Then again, it might only take you a couple of weeks to get the hang of surfing if you immerse yourself.[25]

There are more fascinating things on earth than you could ever get your head round, so you're not going to run out, even if you're limiting yourself to things which you personally enjoy and can afford and manage and fit into your life. There's no excuse or reason to stop.

> # IF THE LEARNING EXPERIENCES AREN'T COMING AT YOU, GET OUT AND FIND THEM

---

[25] Sorry.

RULE 63

You can't turn it off

It's impossible to get through life without learning anything new. To be honest, it's quite hard to get through most days without learning anything. You only need to read a paper or talk to a friend or turn on the TV or go on social media. You might not find all of it useful or even interesting, but there's no shortage of opportunities to learn something new, from the history of the Middle East to celebrity gossip. Even when you already have the skills and knowledge to run your life and do your job, the chance to learn new things keeps coming at you.

Nope, you can't turn it off. But you can turn the volume down. In fact it's an essential skill, because if you engaged with everything you'd pretty soon become overloaded and unable to function. So we all learn to filter the information in order to cope. The trouble is, it's far too easy to mute the incoming information completely. On an everyday level that doesn't interfere with life, but on a broader level it isn't feeding your soul. Learning is what we do as humans, and while you do need to filter out the dross, or indeed the things that aren't dross but really don't interest you at all, it's important to be open to new learning at the same time. That's how you grow.

Let me ask you a question. When was the last time you did an internet search to find out more background to a news story, or discover the meaning of a word you'd just heard, or understand something that had been puzzling you? I hope you can answer this question, because it should be recent enough to remember. It could have been several times already today. (It doesn't have to be the internet of course – you could consult a book, or ask a friend.)

The human condition feeds on new knowledge and learning. It inspires us and gives us reassurance that we're developing and improving and making the most of our time on earth. What's more it keeps us open-minded and stops us becoming reactionary, bigoted, stuck in a fixed mindset. So if you're looking after your own mental and emotional health, it's important that you don't filter out all the everyday opportunities to learn. If you're going through a phase of life where there's no time to enrol on a course or get stuck into serious reading and studying, this may be all you have for a while. Even if you already have time to start your first garden and take an evening class in graphic design, life is still giving you countless chances to feed your brain and find things that interest you and where you don't know everything.

So get into the habit of thinking 'I wonder what the background to this is?' or 'Is this true or just fake news?' or 'Where does that word come from?' or 'I'd like to see some statistics on that' or 'Why does this work like it does?' Then check out the answers. Some might take moments, some might send you down intriguing rabbit holes, and an occasional few might suck you into a whole new area of interest and study. Enjoy!

> # DON'T FILTER OUT ALL THE EVERYDAY OPPORTUNITIES TO LEARN

RULE 64

Reflect

Good – so you're going to start questioning, learning new stuff, finding out more about the things you brush up against as you go through your day. Over time you'll become open-minded, well-informed, interested and interesting. And you'll find life intellectually more rewarding as a result.

Would you like to find it more mentally and emotionally rewarding too? In that case you have to extend the same habit a bit further. Start asking questions about yourself – your experiences, your behaviour, your life. 'Why do I feel this?' and 'Why do I do that?' and 'How has my attitude changed since I was younger?'

We've touched on this earlier in terms of building your resilience, where self-awareness is an important factor. If you make it a habit to question yourself regardless of whether things are going well or not, you'll find it also feeds your need to develop and grow and improve.

I've been around a fair few decades now and when I look back at myself 30 or 40 years ago, I barely recognise me. I'm different in so many ways, and I'm happy with almost all of them.[26] We change hugely through life, and the way to make sure the changes are for the better is to be aware of them, and in control of them. Keep asking yourself about you, and make sure you get answers.

One of the most helpful questions you can ask is, 'What can I learn from this?' When you go through difficult situations, or traumas, or feel you've handled things badly – or indeed well – ask yourself what happened and what you'd do differently next time. Or what you want to make sure to repeat.

If something has made you feel angry or frightened or upset or worried – not feelings that any of us enjoys – it makes sense to ask

---

[26] My family might quibble in some cases, but that's their problem.

yourself how you could feel less angry, frightened, upset, worried next time. Otherwise you can't be surprised when the feelings keep recurring. You might not change your reactions overnight, but over the years you will find you cope better, often way better, than you used to. The same goes for situations that haven't gone well. Reflect on what you could have done differently as a parent, or in your job, or when speaking to your mother, or when you crashed the car.

This isn't rocket science, and I don't understand why everyone doesn't do it as a matter of course. Every night when you go to bed, think about what you've learnt about yourself – or on your daily commute, or when you go for a walk. The bizarrely large number of people who don't do this, don't get much better at coping with life. We all know people who struggle with normal life without any obvious reason, who keep mishandling the same situations, who don't get that if you keep doing the same thing, you'll keep getting the same result. Don't be one of them.

KEEP ASKING YOURSELF ABOUT YOU

PARENTHOOD

It's easy to get lost among the activities and stresses and general busy-ness of being a parent. A lot of the time is spent dealing with minor emergencies, or trying to stay on top of everything, and maybe also juggle work or wider family demands too. To some extent that goes with the territory, and there's a lot to gain from focusing on other people rather than yourself, as we saw right back in Rule 1.

However, you'll be able to do a much more effective job of looking after your family if you're happy in yourself. And while focusing on them will help with that, you can take it too far. Being a parent is supposed to be rewarding. It's not always fun, and some days it's damn hard work, but on balance you should be able to feel content that you're doing it. So you need to look after yourself enough to enjoy your lot, at least on a good day, and so that your children grow up with a broadly relaxed parent who enjoys being around them.

Just to keep you on your toes, the demands of being a parent shift hugely from the sleepless nights with a small baby, to the toddler who never gives you a break, to your school-age child coping with friends and homework, to the teenager who mostly shouts at you and somehow seems more vulnerable than they ever did as an infant. If you have more than one child, and especially if you have, say, a toddler and a teenager, this only gets more complicated and demanding. So finding time for yourself in the midst of it all is a challenge. But that's OK – these next Rules are here to help.

Remember to drain the swamp

When you're up to your neck in alligators, it's hard to remember that the object of the exercise was to drain the swamp. And when you're up to your knees in nappies, it can be similarly hard to remember why you're doing this. Especially when you haven't slept properly in days, months – maybe years – and you have piles of unwashed laundry, unfinished homeworks, and generally unfeasible demands on your time and emotions.

Why did you sign up for this again? Even if it was all a horrible mistake and you never actually put your name on the dotted line, why are you doing it? Everyone talks about the delight of having children, but there are plenty of days when it's hard to find the joy. Days when you just feel like a drudge, an unpaid servant, a skivvy. Days when it really doesn't feel as if you're doing this for *you* – more like everyone else.

This may be normal, but it's no fun. So it really helps to remind yourself as often as possible what the point of it is from your perspective. The more often you can do this, the better, but aim for a minimum of once a day. Time you dedicate properly to doing the wonderful bits of being a parent instead of the hard work. When you're lucky, these moments arrive of their own accord. Sometimes they come thick and fast, and sometimes they're thin on the ground. What really helps is to be aware of them when they happen, to consciously tell yourself, 'This is great – this is what it's all about.'

And be pro-active about it. If those joyous moments don't present themselves, generate them yourself. Even if it's only five minutes a day, make sure you spend some time enjoying being a parent, and consciously appreciating it. Give yourself permission to leave the laundry and the drudgery alone for a bit, and just immerse yourself in the moment.

Which bit of parenting do you most enjoy? Personally, my favourite bit has always been snuggling up at bedtime reading them a story. Unfortunately, the teenagers don't seem to appreciate it, but the younger ones love it. No matter what sort of day you've had, you can put all the worry or exhaustion to one side and remind yourself why you're doing this. It doesn't have to be the bedtime book though – or better still it can be other times as well as story time. The key is to put everything else out of your mind and just live in the present (Rule 39).

Every child is different, and every age is different. For you and your child – at the moment – it might be a trip to the park, or drawing at the kitchen table, or watching a favourite TV pro-gramme together (if you have a child who still watches TV – there are fewer of those around these days). I've had small children who loved bath time, and ones who hated it, and ones who loved it but threw major tantrums when it was time to stop (which made it less fun as a parent). If your child loves it, that's another great time to reflect on what fun it is being a parent.

You need to be flexible as your child gets older, and find your moments doing new things. The great thing is that the more you can do this, the better you get at noticing how much you're enjoy-ing the good bits whenever they happen. And the more times a day you can think 'Wow! This is lovely!' the happier you'll feel in the between-times while you wash the nappies and sort out the squabbles and tidy up the toys.

> **THE MORE YOU CAN DO THIS, THE BETTER YOU GET AT NOTICING HOW MUCH YOU'RE ENJOYING THE GOOD BITS**

Nobody's perfect

One of the most soul-destroying things about being a parent can be the guilt, the feeling that you messed up, the realisation that you should have handled something better. At the end of the day, when the kids are in bed, you go over your day and feel you've let yourself down by being irritable, or not listening to them properly, or forgetting to make them wear a coat, or making them go to school even though they weren't feeling great.

We've all been there, and it's pointless. It makes you feel worse, without making the kids feel any better. Sure, a bit of practical reviewing can be handy (note to self: if it's snowing suggest they wear a coat),[27] but the negative emotions – the sense of inadequacy, failure, guilt – they're not helping anyone. So dump them, and focus on tomorrow.

If you can point out a parent who has never made any mistakes, even when no one was looking, please let me know. Good luck finding them as I never have. And actually, can you imagine how miserable it would be to grow up with parents who were flawless? You'd feel forever inadequate as a child. And you'd get no experience of being around people who were a bit tetchy or forgetful or bossy or momentarily humourless, or indeed set an example for how to apologise when they got it wrong. That's no grounding for adult life. Your kids need you to be human, so they can be human too.

When you have these times of self-doubt, there are three things that help. Firstly, register what you feel you could do better next time, as a practical pointer, not an emotional stick to beat yourself up with. Recognise, for example, that if your child tries to

---

[27] I have genuinely made this mistake – we could see snow up on the moors but down where we were it was still mild as I bundled the kids into the car with promises of building a snowman. It turned out that snow is actually quite a lot colder than it looks from a distance.

talk to you seriously when you're really busy, it doesn't work. So resolve that next time it happens you either stop what you're doing, or you ask the child to wait until you can give them your full attention. That's a useful memo for the future that sees today's experience as an opportunity to learn, not to berate yourself.

Secondly, remind yourself of the bigger picture. You're trying to get them to the age of 18 in one piece, and with the basic skills they need to start the rest of their life. That's it. In the grand scheme of things, spread over those 18 years, how much does it really matter that you were a bit ratty today, or that you forgot to buy bread, or that you didn't realise snow would be cold? It's just not important enough to give yourself a hard time over. Most times, no one will ever even remember (or they'll thoroughly enjoy relating the story of when dad took them out to build a snowman *without coats*).[28]

Thirdly, look back over your day and notice all the things you got right. The kids had clean clothes, and everyone enjoyed walking the dog, and the shopping got done, and lunch tasted good, and bath time was fun. Those are only examples, but if you've managed that much on one day you're doing really well. If you're going to appraise where there's room for improvement, it's only right that you should also review your successes. That's just good practice after all.

> # YOUR KIDS NEED YOU TO BE HUMAN, SO THEY CAN BE HUMAN TOO

---

[28] Oh alright, I admit it ... also without hats, gloves, scarves ... .

Know yourself

Following on from the last Rule, there are one-off mistakes and then there are trends, let's call them. Anyone can be forgiven for the hiccups, especially if you learn from them so you're less likely to repeat them, or at least you repeat them less often than you would without the 'review and learn' approach.

It's important to understand yourself as a parent, so you can also spot where certain types of behaviour are getting to be a bit of a habit. If you don't like that behaviour, you need to analyse it in order to reduce the habit, because while we all lapse from time to time, in the end the days add up. You'll be more comfortable in your own skin if you feel your plusses outweigh any minuses, so it's important you do this so you can relax and enjoy being a parent (in as much as you can ever relax).

To give you an example, I know a few parents who spend quite a lot of their time angry. This is their natural personality for whatever reason, but it has a tendency to come out in their parenting. Now up to a point, children can perfectly happily grow up accepting that mum can be a bit shouty, or dad is quite often curt – clearly there's a point where this tips over into abuse, but that's not the case with these parents I know. They just have a short fuse. However, if you're one of those parents and you don't want to be, you first have to recognise and acknowledge it. Then you have to address it. You won't change it overnight, but you can work on it, on your own or with your partner or a friend or a therapist. There's lots you can do to modify your behaviour and to avoid some of the triggers, but only once you've been honest with yourself and recognised the behaviour.

I've known parents with a clear tendency to be distracted and never quite listen properly, or to sulk at their kids, or to criticise them, or put pressure on them to get good grades, or to praise them too much – or never – or to over-protect them, or to be controlling. We all do a bit of some of these things, some of the time. It's normal. But if you don't like the frequency of one of your less attractive habits, noticing it is the first step to changing it.

Look, this isn't about trying to be someone you're not. Some of us will always be better at reading stories than at tinkering under a car bonnet with the kids, or more cut out for playing sport with them than playing chess. No one can do everything, and your kids will accept that, and learn that it means they don't have to be perfect at everything either. This is about your behaviour, not your personality. If you don't like your own tendency towards snapping, or criticising, or ignoring your children, these are things you can work on and improve.

As before, please also observe your good habits. If you are almost always patient, recognise it and give yourself a pat on the back. Or maybe you're reliably kind to your children. Or a good listener, or great at having a laugh, or fair-minded, or consistent ... being self-aware means understanding the positives too and seeing them set against anything you would like to change.

> ## THIS IS ABOUT YOUR BEHAVIOUR, NOT YOUR PERSONALITY

Trust your own judgement

It's funny how ready people are to give you advice about how to bring up your children. And when I say funny, obviously what I mean is not funny. Just infuriating. My view is that unless you're specifically asked, you should never give out parenting advice.[29] Anyone who knows enough to give any kind of opinion should be perfectly aware that every child, every parent and every family is different. So what works for them won't necessarily work for anyone else.

If you have any lack of self-confidence in your skills as a parent, it's very easy to feel undermined by your mother or your friend or some parent at the school gates telling you what you should be doing differently. Perhaps you're too soft on your child? Maybe you're including too much meat in their diet? What if they ought to be going to bed earlier? Are they really the only child in their class without their own phone?

One of the best ways to look after yourself as a parent, to keep a positive attitude, is to develop a set of blinkers. Just focus on your own child and think rationally through what works for them – and you – and don't pay any attention to what everyone else is doing. You can peek out occasionally to see if you notice any good ideas that might work for you, but otherwise do things your way. Any unsolicited advice should be either ignored, or taken as a vague suggestion and no more.

The system that works best for your family is going to include a reasonable level of conformity, because being completely out of kilter with society isn't going to be the best thing for your child

---

[29] By reading this section you are deemed to have specifically asked, so I'm allowed to write this.

when you're deciding how to raise them. If everyone else at school wears uniform, the best option will be for your child to wear the same uniform. So doing things your way won't put you at odds with the rest of the world.

One friend of mine has a child who is quite socially anxious and used to find parties very daunting. So my friend went with her to birthday parties for a while, and then stayed for the first few minutes before quietly disappearing, and worked up to the point of simply dropping his daughter off and leaving her. It worked well for them. But it might not work for your socially anxious child. In fact it might make things worse. Your child might need to delay going to parties at all until she's a bit older, or to be thrown in at the deep end from the start and just dropped off to fend for herself. Only you know which will work, and it might take a bit of trial and error to work it out. No one else can tell you, based on their experience, what you should do.

And that goes for pocket money, how often you bath the kids, whether you let your teenager have a computer in their bedroom, or anything else. And it's fine to fit it all around whether you yourself can cope with early mornings, or bedtime squabbles, or having your mother look after the kids. You need to feel sane in order to keep on top of those things. So trust your own parental judgement, and when anyone else tells you what to do just say, 'Thanks, I'll bear that in mind' and then carry on as you were.

> ## ONE OF THE BEST WAYS TO LOOK AFTER YOURSELF AS A PARENT IS TO DEVELOP A SET OF BLINKERS

Be honest with yourself

You might have noticed that all these Rules about looking after yourself as a parent involve an element of being honest with yourself. If you just get swept along in the day-to-day it's much harder to enjoy the process. A bit of reflection and rational thought, which you can do while you're shopping or commuting or laundering even when life is busy, makes all the difference. If you're not happy with your lot, you need to change it. So obviously you have to work out which bits want changing.

Sometimes it's perfectly clear which bits don't work, and it's easy to identify and deal with them. It might be obvious that the bedtime routine needs to start 15 minutes earlier, or shopping twice a week would work much better than every other day.

However some of the things that need to change require an uncomfortable level of honesty. Maybe you hate playing board games – but your child loves it and asks you to play with them on a daily basis. Are you going to go on putting up with it, or will you find an alternative – either an alternative activity, or an alternative person who isn't you to play the board games? Pretty straightforward and solvable, but it's not always easy to admit that you don't enjoy playing with your child. So be honest – with yourself, you don't have to make a public confession – and acknowledge that you love playing with your child, except when it's board games. It's OK, we've all been there.

Here's a tougher one. Suppose you have a favourite child? Lots of parents don't, but many do. Definitely don't admit it to your children, obviously, but it's important you're honest with yourself. It's much easier to keep the fact hidden if you're aware of it, because then you can monitor your attitudes to them to make sure it doesn't show.

Having a favourite child often says more about the parent than the children themselves – some parents prefer one child because they're easy, or because that child is more needy and the parent likes being needed, so think about why they're your favourite. And even whether they really are your favourite: it's quite easy to like one child better while *loving* them equally. Or to prefer one because you naturally hang out together. However, deliberately spending time with the other child can sometimes redress that balance. See – none of these options are possible if you're not honest with yourself.

And here's another scenario where honesty is vital: if you're struggling to cope. There should always be some kind of help available from somewhere – family, friends, online groups, charities, the state – but only if you ask. And you can't ask until you realise you need that support. So level with yourself if you're struggling. And if you find it difficult to ask for help, be honest with yourself about that too. Why is it difficult? What will happen if you don't ask? What are your alternatives?

All parents need help, and the only ones who don't ask are the ones who already have that help on tap one way or another. They'd be asking too if they didn't have a creche at work, or a friend to share childcare with, or family living around the corner, or enough money to pay for a cleaner or childminder or au pair.

> # SOME OF THE THINGS THAT NEED TO CHANGE REQUIRE AN UNCOMFORTABLE LEVEL OF HONESTY

Communicate

Unless you're a single parent, there are two of you in this. Sometimes all the family jobs get divvied up and the parent who is responsible for bringing in the income doesn't do much of the childcare stuff. In other families the tasks are split differently so maybe both parents earn, perhaps one cooks and the other deals with the laundry, maybe one does the bulk of the childcare during the week and the other at the weekend. Any and all permutations are possible, and all are fine so long as everyone is happy with the arrangement.

But are you happy with the arrangement? Is it working for you? Sometimes these agreements are made before the first child arrives, and no one really knows what it's like to have children until they're there. Maybe it worked brilliantly with toddlers, but now the kids are teenagers one of you is working much harder than the other. Which you might or might not still be happy with.

I know a couple who agreed that when they had kids they'd both work but she'd fit her work round the children and look after them too. It made sense as his work was high-powered and very highly paid, and hers wasn't. Unfortunately two of the children had a serious medical condition that took a lot of managing, so she had to stop working altogether. Eventually, as the kids got older, it became possible for her to go back to work. She started a small business which took off fantastically, and he cut back on work, but she continued also to cope with all the childcare because as far as he was concerned, that was the deal, and she didn't argue with that. But it was a deal that had never taken into account the unexpected circumstances they found themselves in.

And the moral of this is: communicate with each other. Children keep growing and changing, and so do the demands of being a parent. If you have a partner – or indeed a mother or brother or friend who is closely involved in raising your kids – you have to work as a team. And good teams communicate.

My friends had a huge issue they should have communicated about better, because one of them ended up frazzled and run off her feet while the other just failed to realise how unbalanced their inputs had become. But even your day-to-day life runs more easily and smoothly if you talk to each other about the little glitches and gripes. Not only the practical things – 'If you only do the laundry at the weekend there are no clean socks for the kids by Friday' – but also the emotional ones. The fact that you feel you've got an unfair share of the worst jobs, or that you really need a couple of hours to yourself by the weekend, or that you're finding one of the kids a struggle to get on with just at the moment, or that if you have to make up another school lunch box you think you'll explode.

Your partner (or mother/brother/friend) won't know how you're feeling if you don't tell them, so don't give them a hard time. Just raise it as you would at work (I hope) in a practical manner as a problem you'd like to work through and solve together. And remember to reciprocate – listen constructively and do your best to help when your partner tells you they need your help. Once boundaries have been reset, it's important to hold each other to the new arrangements – not always easy but without constructive changes the communication is hollow.

> YOUR PARTNER WON'T KNOW
> HOW YOU'RE FEELING IF YOU
> DON'T TELL THEM

Nurture your relationship

Some days it's hard to see your way through until bedtime, let alone beyond that. But one day your work as a parent will be done. Oh OK, no it won't. It's never done. But one day the children leave home and being a parent becomes a very different job. And who will be left in the house? Just you and your partner. How's that going to be? (There's more on this by the way, whether you're single or with a partner, in Rule 87.)

I hope the idea excites you. I hope you feel that it will be like it was before the kids came along, that you'll be able to do all those things together that you both enjoy and don't have time for now. But you're going to need more than hope to make that work. You're going to need to keep the connection, the spark, the love you had at the start.

Too many couples spend 18 years or so with their heads down, getting through each day as it comes, focused on the kids. This might be a hard grind or it might be thoroughly enjoyable – probably a bit of each at times. However the result is that when the kids leave, the couple barely know each other any more and can't remember why they got together. They might have made really effective colleagues for the last 18 years, a good team, but now their joint project is all but completed, they can no longer see a reason to be together.

Some couples work hard to remedy this, while others feel it's too late. But even if you do manage to reclaim what you had before, how much easier if you'd never lost it in the first place. And actually, how much more fun those child-rearing years would have been if you'd done it all while still experiencing the feeling of your heart skipping a beat when the other one walked into the room.

There's another reason, too, why you need to stay in love with each other. Your children haven't spent 18 years in the same house as you without noticing how you relate to each other. And they need to be free to leave home. It's so much easier for them to go when they can see you'll be fine – better than fine – without them there.

In the end your relationship with your partner is more important than the one with your children, because the children need it to be too. They have to see that you have a stronger focus than them. I'm not saying you should love anyone more or less – that would be impossible and unnecessary – but your children will find their own partners eventually. Partners who will be even more important to them than you are, and that's as it should be. Meanwhile you and your partner might have decades still left to spend together, and the happier those years are, the better for everyone.

So don't keep thinking you'll spend time together next week or next month, or you'll work on the relationship once your youngest goes to school. Procrastination is a dangerous enemy here. Communicate, spend time alone together, keep your sex life alive – even if it's not quite as energetic as it once was – find things to laugh about together, and do it now. Right now.

> **YOUR RELATIONSHIP WITH YOUR PARTNER IS MORE IMPORTANT THAN THE ONE WITH YOUR CHILDREN**

RULE 72

Stay healthy

Being a parent can be challenging at times, much more so if you're feeling below par to start with. It's natural as a parent to put your child first, and to worry about their health before yours. On many levels this is the way it works when you have kids. Of course we all keep on going through coughs and sniffles – what alternative do we have? And generally there's no point complaining because, with the best will in the world, a toddler just doesn't care if you have a headache or feel a bit sick. You might get a bit of sympathy from your 10-year-old, but by their teens they're back to not caring again, because obviously their problems are *so* much worse than yours.

There's not much you can do about coughs and colds, but it's important that you do your best to stay healthy as a parent. There may not be time to make yourself a healthy fresh squeezed juice every morning, and you might have to lay off your personal trainer, or put the triathlon practice on hold, or cut down the time you spend in yoga classes. Nevertheless it's all too easy to go to the other extreme. Time is in short supply, and time without a child in tow may be even harder to find, and many parents give up on their own wellbeing altogether.

However, children need parents who are as healthy as possible, because they need your energy. How can they sap it if it you don't have any? So even if you're inclined to be a martyr and to ignore your own health in favour of theirs, remember that you're looking after yourself for them as well as you. You may have chronic health problems to manage, in which case you have my sympathy – that must be hugely challenging as a parent. You don't have to be the healthiest parent in the world though – just the healthiest *you* can be.

In all honesty, when your kids are small they'll keep you pretty fit without much extra input from you. You'll be forever jumping up to fetch them things, running to catch them before they plummet down steps, lifting them in and out of trolleys and high chairs and car seats. They make a pretty efficient fitness tool. This does wear off eventually though, and you still need to make sure you stay reasonably fit.

Crucially, you need to eat properly. This is vital to your physical health, and something it's too easy to forget as a parent. You don't want to eat at 5.30pm so you decide you'll eat after they've gone to bed. But when the time comes, you can't be bothered so you just grab a lump of cheese or a couple of biscuits or some toast. Once is fine, but it gets to be habit far too quickly. So be strict with yourself about eating plenty of fresh vegetables and all the other things that are good for you. It's a good example to be setting too.

Then there's your mental health, and goodness knows your children need you to be as emotionally resilient as you can manage. So milk all the Rules in this book about relaxation and resilience as much as you can, to be sure you're in the best place to have fun with the kids, and to muster the energy to say no to them when necessary and cope with the fallout. Everyone has a different experience, but I know plenty of parents who will tell you that the emotional side of being a parent gets tougher as the physical demands start to reduce. Toddlers have nothing on teenagers when it comes to emotional needs.

CHILDREN NEED PARENTS WHO ARE AS HEALTHY AS POSSIBLE, BECAUSE THEY NEED YOUR ENERGY. HOW CAN THEY SAP IT IF YOU DON'T HAVE ANY?

AT WORK

When things are going well, work can be uplifting, energising, exciting, fulfilling, stimulating. Ah, but it's not always like that, is it? Some jobs can be frustrating, difficult, exhausting, or just plain boring. Even the best of them can feel like hard work if the rest of your life isn't going well.

Work occupies a huge amount of our waking time, so if we want to take care of ourselves we need to make sure that we're working in the healthiest way possible. That means our mental as well as our physical health. Not only will that make the 40-odd hours a week at work more enjoyable and easier, it will also feed back into your general wellbeing the rest of the time, when you're not at work.

Some people work hugely long hours with lots of travel, emails flying around at all hours of day and night, weekend working, breakfast meetings, high pressure. These kind of high stress jobs work brilliantly for some people, and not at all for others. The biggest factor is how much you actually enjoy it – if the whole mad crazy thing gives you a massive buzz, you'll cope far better. Also if you can focus on your job without other distractions it makes a huge difference – living for your work is much easier when you're young and free than it is when you have a family who would like to see you from time to time.

If you have this kind of job and you love it, don't let me stop you. However, if you're not happy with your work, it will affect your health detrimentally, and a high stress job you don't actually like is far worse than a few hours of part-time routine each week. So whatever job you do, and however many hours you work, make sure the effort you put in is commensurate with the pleasure you get out of it. We can't all have the most exciting jobs, and the Rules in this section will ensure – even if your work is underwhelming – that you stay as happy and healthy as possible.

Stay motivated

Anything is more fun if you have a good reason to be doing it. Enough incentive makes anything worthwhile. If your job is already thoroughly enjoyable, and you look forward to it every morning when you wake up, that's great. However not many people are that lucky, and most of us have times when we just don't want to be at work. That might not even be work's fault – it could be because your relationship is going through a bad patch, or you're worried about money, or one of your friends is seriously ill.

Then again, some jobs go through bad patches of their own – a new boss, or a change of work practices, or a gruelling seasonal rush of orders – which mean they're more effort than they used to be for less apparent return. You can find yourself going through the motions to get through the day until you can go home again.

If this is how you're feeling about work, you've lost your motivation. Perhaps understandably, but you need to do something about it because in the long term those feelings of frustration or boredom or general lack of enthusiasm will start to get to you. Your mental health will suffer, and maybe your physical health along with it.

One of the keys is to remember why you're there at all. What are the good parts of the job? What are you getting out of it in terms of money, career, friendships? Focus on the longer-term benefits, rather than on the immediate task. Lift your eyes up above the mundane chores and see the bigger picture. Perhaps the processes are boring, but you're surrounded by colleagues who are real friends. Or maybe the money is great. Or the hours fit perfectly around the rest of your life. Or this is the step you need up the career ladder.

If you honestly can't find a reason for doing your job that makes it worthwhile, you might even need to question why you're there at all. If it's not the money, presumably you either don't need it, or can earn it elsewhere. Sometimes we lose long-term motivation because, actually, the job really isn't doing it for us any longer. If that's the case, you should seriously consider quitting and doing something else. No, I'm not advising you to leave the job – I'm advising you to consider leaving. Think about what it would mean for you, and what else you could do. The prospect of leaving may suddenly help you to see why you want to stay – and there's your motivation.

Or it might be that this isn't the career for you any more. I have a friend who got out of banking to become a teacher, another who switched from corporate marketing to become a therapist, and one who left publishing to run a charity. Goodness knows I've had a fair few careers myself over a lifetime. And all of us have moved because, for whatever reason, we no longer felt the motivation to stay.

> **FOCUS ON THE LONGER-TERM BENEFITS, RATHER THAN ON THE IMMEDIATE TASK**

RULE 74

Don't up the ante

Here's a Rule for the committed, the driven, the perfectionists. That can be a lot of us at some times and in some areas of life. For example it's me at work, but not me when it comes to housework. What happens is that you set yourself a goal and then, as you start to get close to it – which you will because you're so committed, driven, perfectionist – you move the goalposts further away. By never allowing yourself to reach the goal, you can never really achieve success.

The risk, whether at work or elsewhere, is that you demotivate yourself and thus become frustrated, and even susceptible to burnout. Given how much time you spend at work, this has the potential to bring you down considerably, and to leach all the fun out of the job. There's never any opportunity to sit back and enjoy your success, because you're still pushing on. And if you do complete a project you home in on what you could have done better, rather than acknowledging the success of the overall picture.

Even if you struggle to recognise this in yourself, you must have seen it in other people, who keep raising the bar so that they can never actually clear it. If you take that metaphor literally, it can be quite common in athletes. As soon as they realise they can clear the bar, or run a mile in four minutes, they immediately want to raise the bar again, or run a mile in 3 minutes 55.

Now listen, I know you get real pleasure from the challenge. I understand that you'd be miserable if you lowered your standards. I get that it's important to you to keep pushing yourself. And all of that is fine, so long as it makes you happy. But for too many people, it stops making them happy, while the alternative – not caring, not trying – would make them more miserable.

So here's a solution for all those perfectionists in danger of burning out or being made miserable by their excessive demands on themselves. Make it a Rule that you never raise the bar. Once you have set yourself a goal, work hard towards that goal, and when you get there – drum roll please – stop. Just stop. Stop and look back at what you have achieved, and feel pleased with yourself. Acknowledge your success. Congratulate yourself.

OK. All done? Feeling properly pleased and successful? Enjoyed your basking in glory moment? Good, well done. You deserved it. *Now* you can set yourself a fresh target, and start up again working towards that. It should be obvious that this won't change what you achieve in the longer term at all. You're still going bigger and better. The only difference is in your attitude. Now you can feel successful and have a moment – or an evening, or a weekend or whatever is appropriate – to feel positive about yourself.

Similarly, if you've just completed a really successful product launch, for example, give yourself time to sit back and enjoy the feeling, and to reflect on how smoothly it went, how well the team worked, how much interest there was from customers. Plenty of time tomorrow or next week to review whether there was anything you could learn to make the next launch go even better still. For now, you can't learn to repeat what you got right unless you recognise that too. And if you lead a team, they need to hear you acknowledge the achievement.

MAKE IT A RULE THAT YOU

NEVER RAISE THE BAR

Create boundaries

If you have a colleague, or indeed a mother or a friend, who always does anything you ask of them happily, you're going to keep asking, aren't you? I mean, why wouldn't you? You need the help, and it doesn't seem to bother them, so of course you're going to see if they could just cover for you for a few minutes, or cast their eye over this report, or have a word with the boss on your behalf. Or in the case of family and friends you might ask them to pick up some shopping for you while they're out, or to mind the kids for a few minutes.

That works both ways round. If you're similarly happy to help other people, they're much more likely to ask you. And up to a point, that's fine. The thing is, they don't know where that point is – the point beyond which it isn't fine. Only you know that. So you need to let them know too, or they'll be asking for things that aren't really OK.

Also, that point moves around, so one day it might be easy to cover for your colleague but tomorrow it might not. How are they meant to understand that? I'll tell you: they aren't meant to, and they won't. If you agree to stay late at work today, your boss *will* assume it's OK to ask you again next week. Yes, even if you did lamely say 'just this once'. They won't hear that bit – that's human nature. So you need clear ground rules, and you need to stick to them. Yes, even on the days when it really is fine to help out, because you don't want to set a precedent.

Of course it's great to be as helpful as you can to other people within your parameters, and you choose what those parameters are. Maybe you need a good 30 minutes for lunch but not the whole hour. Maybe you're genuinely happy to stay late occasionally, so long as it's no later than 6pm. Or only in the few days running up to a big presentation or exhibition or event. Establish your parameters in cold blood, not in the heat of the moment. Know in advance what you will and won't say no to. For example you might be firm about working only 9–5, or not checking emails in the evening or at weekends. It's definitely good for your mental health to insist that your annual leave is a total break from work with no checking of emails at all. Another excellent rule is that you won't ever take work home with you – that one can turn into a very slippery slope.

I realise that some of these suggestions are going to sound completely ridiculous if you work in, say, a high-pressure job in the City, where it's taken as read that you'll work late every evening and be on call 24/7. I'll be frank, I don't approve of asking that much of employees in any job, but I know it happens. Nevertheless there will still be colleagues who are more put-upon than others, and you need to make sure you're not one of them. If you love the job, that's fine. If it doesn't make you happy, you might want to talk to your boss about parameters that could work for you both, if they don't you want you to either leave or burn out somewhere down the line.

> # IF YOU AGREE TO STAY LATE AT WORK TODAY, YOUR BOSS *WILL* ASSUME IT'S OK TO ASK YOU AGAIN NEXT WEEK

RULE 76

Have switch-off time

The last Rule was about the boundaries you set when you're at work, primarily for other people to follow. And look, these ground rules are for you, as well as your colleagues. You can easily persuade yourself to stay late, or to cover for someone else, unless you too understand that an inch will soon turn into a mile, and staying late once will gradually turn into once a week, and then maybe more.

It's vital for your health that there are times when you don't work. Ideally, that will be all the times you're not actually at work, but not all jobs are quite like that, and not all people. If you want to go over papers on your morning commute, that's fine.[30] And checking in once or twice when you're at home might be OK, if it works for you. But you have to be sure it will consistently work for you. You don't want to get into a habit that is fine some days but can really stress you on others – if you're busy at home, or on the occasions when you pick up a depressing or concerning email.

And this Rule becomes absolutely vital if you work from home, either permanently or occasionally. If you run your own business from home, you need this Rule more than anyone. If you break the rule not to work in the evenings once, it's so much harder not to break it again. And again. Many years ago, when I was young and single, I could work until 2am from home and no one cared, least of all me. Once I had a family though, it simply wasn't fair on them if I spent a whole evening working (as was pointed out to me). So I adopted the policy that I didn't work after 6pm or at weekends.

So you need to fit your ground rules to your situation, and recognise that this may change. The important thing is that you switch off from work because it's much healthier to have a clear mental

---

[30] As long as you don't drive to work.

separation between work and home, and that's impossible if you blur all the boundaries.

When everything is going swimmingly at work, you might really enjoy immersing yourself in it outside official working hours (though your family may not). But things never go well all the time, and the problem with blurring the boundaries is not just that you bring your paperwork or emails into your home life, but that you also bring with it the worries, anxieties, fears and concerns that go with it. Those are the bits you really need to switch off, and while it will always be a challenge when there are major work problems, it can only be harder if there's no mental separation between work and home.

This plays the other way round too: if things are tough at home for any reason, work can be an escape, somewhere you can go and put your home worries to the back of your mind for a bit. And again, that only works when you're already in the habit of keeping the two apart.

> IT'S MUCH HEALTHIER TO HAVE
> A CLEAR MENTAL SEPARATION
> BETWEEN WORK AND HOME

Be flexible

In the UK, and in many other countries, it's becoming easier to ask for flexible working arrangements.[31] Employers don't have to say yes (they need specific grounds to say no) but you have a right to ask, and actually this is a cultural thing too. It means it's accepted that people can work flexibly, and that it often benefits the employer too in terms of reduced costs and increased productivity.

Of course it's always been possible to work flexibly, and anyone can *ask* even if it used to be harder to get your boss to agree to it. Now that it's on the increase though, it's worth considering it if traditional working hours are putting a strain on you. It doesn't matter whether your need is logistical or emotional – flexible working can be a great way to stay healthy and happy at work.

Circumstances change, and just because you had no need to work flexibly last year or five years ago, doesn't mean it wouldn't help you now. It doesn't matter whether it's because you can't find anyone to mind the kids after school, or because you're much happier working alone, or because you want to be able to take the occasional long weekend. So long as your employer is still getting as much value out of you as before – if not more – it's entirely reasonable to propose it.

So be creative. Being flexible isn't only about hours. Certainly you could ask to start and finish work earlier, or work through lunch and leave earlier, but there are other options too. It's about what works for you, without short-changing your company. I had a boss once who offered me the option of shortening all my lunch breaks in exchange for every third Monday off. I had the option to say no, but actually I grabbed the chance of a regular long weekend.

---

[31] One of the few good things to come out of Covid-19.

You might ask to stick to your normal working hours but spend some days at home, or working from a different office. You could even ask to work part-time for a pro rata reduction in salary – it's not for everyone, but it could be exactly what you need right now. Or you could ask to switch roles in order to be more flexible. A back office job, for example, might give you more scope for working flexibly than a customer-facing one.

This is all about keeping you as well and as happy as possible, and if work is getting in the way of that, you need to do something about it. So work out what that thing is, and ask for it. Obviously in some roles it's not practical to work from home, or in the evenings, but if your company values you they should see the benefit in finding an arrangement that works for both of you, and not just for them.

And remember you can change your working hours even if you work from home. If you hate early starts, maybe shift your working time to fit, just as I once worked until 2am and now always stop at 6pm. I know one person who works long hours four days a week instead of doing five 8-hour days, and her employer is quite happy with it. So think flexibly about how to optimise your time and place of work for everyone's benefit.

> ## BE CREATIVE. BEING FLEXIBLE ISN'T ONLY ABOUT HOURS

Stay in synch

Are you one of those people who wakes up and, bang, you're into your day? You check your emails before you get out of bed, think about your first meeting while you're still in the shower, wolf down a piece of toast on your way out of the door? Lots of us do it. We're barely aware of ourselves going through the motions of washing, dressing, breakfasting, because our mind is an hour ahead of our body.

It's so easy to do, especially when life is busy or work is demanding. But you're really not living in the present, are you (Rule **39**)? You might think you work an eight-hour day, but you can stick another hour or two on to the beginning of that. And mostly a fairly unproductive couple of hours, too. How much can you honestly achieve while you're showering, or cleaning your teeth? Is that email really so urgent that your reply couldn't wait until 9am?

It's when work is stressful or challenging that it's most important you don't do this. You're giving yourself no breathing space, no time to relax and chill at the start of the day, and you're not even achieving much either. So keep your mind where your body is. Think home thoughts. Focus on enjoying your shower or your breakfast or your partner or kids.

You don't have to get up any earlier to do this – goodness knows, I'm not one to advise anyone to get up earlier than they have to. Nope, not a morning person, me. So unless you want to, you don't need to change your routine. It's just about where your mind is while you're doing it. Worrying about the bits of the day that haven't happened yet is not only fruitless but also bad for your mental health.

In an ideal world, you won't start thinking about work until you get there. After all, they don't pay you until you get there, so why should you? Read a book on your commuter train, listen to a podcast in the car, enjoy the weather as you walk or cycle. I appreciate that there will be the occasional one-off day when you want to prepare mentally for a big interview or presentation that day, but that should be a rare occasion, and one where you use the time really productively – to plan or rehearse, not to worry and fret.

Are you still worrying about that email you can't reply to until 9am? Well, don't. For a start you don't know it exists because you're not looking at your emails before you arrive at work, remember. And here's part two of keeping your body and mind synchronised: when you get to work, give yourself time to get up to speed. If you have any control over your day, schedule 30 minutes or an hour clear to prepare for the day and get anything urgent out of the way. So *now* you can check your emails.

Your colleagues will learn that you're not available before 9.30am unless it's urgent. If your workplace kicks off on the dot and there's not much you can do about it, try getting in half an hour early so you can get your head round the day in peace before it starts. Oh alright, you might have to get up a bit earlier – for which you have my undiluted sympathy – but you know what? You'll feel so much better for it. I've had to do it myself in some jobs and (whisper it) it's still worth it.

> # IN AN IDEAL WORLD, YOU WON'T START THINKING ABOUT WORK UNTIL YOU GET THERE

Enjoy your surroundings

It's surprising the difference it makes to your mental health if you like the space where you work. As a space to be in. Unless you're hot desking, or working in a shared space such as a shop floor, you should have at least some control over your working environment. And actually if you are moving about all the time it matters a bit less anyway.

So take some joy and pride in your desk. Personalise it. Just keeping it tidy can make a big difference, as can putting a family photo or two on it, or a favourite mascot. It appeals to our most basic instincts to mark our territory like this, and consequently it's very satisfying and makes you feel you belong, as well as being aesthetically pleasing. Even without a desk, you can take it on yourself to spruce up the staff room or other shared area, or bring a favourite photo to put out when hot desking.

The best thing of all to bring you health and happiness is living plants. There's a lot of research to show that sharing your workspace with plants is good for your wellbeing – they boost creativity and productivity, reduce stress, and improve the air quality. And that's before you consider how they brighten the place up visually. No, not rubbishy plastic plants that gather dust – it has to be the real thing. Yes, you will have to water them. However, many indoor plants are very easy to care for, and pretty tolerant about how often they get watered. Ask around or get advice to make sure you choose plants that are a comfortable fit with your capability to look after them.

If you have enough control over your space, stand back and look at it properly. Is this actually the best place for your desk? Would you rather be able to see out of the window when you're working? Could you clear some space for a plant on top of the filing cabinet? Is there room to hang a picture on the wall – not a year planner or a work certificate, but an actual picture of some kind that you actually enjoy looking at?

Getting your surroundings right is really crucial when you work from home. It's hard to feel motivated when your desk is squeezed into a gap under the stairs between the dirty laundry and the recycling bin. If you spend most of your time here, it's a really high priority that you create a space – however compact – that you actually like. Make sure you can get at everything easily, without having to move the laundry to reach it, so your work flows more smoothly and without unnecessary frustrations. If there really isn't a better place to put your desk, at least relocate the laundry and the recycling.

If you can possibly manage it, have a home workspace which is separate from the rest of the house. In the attic or garage or spare bedroom or landing, but not in the rooms you use when you're not at work. Remember that you need to be able to switch off at the end of the day and at weekends (Rule 76) and that's really hard if your desk is in the kitchen or the living room. Even the smallest cupboard plus a chair can be a really enjoyable space if you give it some thought, and it can transform your attitude to your day.

> # THE BEST THING OF ALL TO BRING YOU HEALTH AND HAPPINESS IS LIVING PLANTS

RULE 80

Create order

How do the words 'time management' make you feel? Some people take huge delight in being organised and efficient, while the phrase strikes dread, guilt and misery into other people. We're all different, and there's no shame in not being naturally organised. However if you want to look after yourself at work, if you want to end every day feeling satisfied rather than frazzled, this is the key to achieving it. It's so much easier to feel calm and ordered on the inside if your external world is calm and ordered.

I know I spend a lot of time advising you to live in the moment, and I stand by that – it's a real shortcut to avoiding unnecessary stress and worry. However, it doesn't work when it comes to the practicalities of work. If you don't plan ahead, organise, schedule, you spend your whole working day firefighting. Tasks that should have been minor two weeks ago become crises because you didn't deal with them and they've turned into monsters. Time is wasted looking for things that aren't where they should be, or apologising to people for things you still haven't done. Your inbox gets ever bigger and other people get frustrated and take it out on you. Familiar?

And it's not actually fun, is it? So why are you doing it to yourself? If you find work stressful on a normal day, how on earth do you manage on a genuinely busy and frenetic day? And listen, it's not as if the answer is even difficult to see. Don't take my word for it. Look around you at the people who are organised and the ones that aren't, and work it out for yourself.

The biggest barrier to becoming organised is that if you're the kind of person who can't deal with their inbox, the idea of getting on top of your entire working life just looks too daunting. Hang on though, that doesn't actually make sense. Because the alternative is running to catch up with yourself , stressed and frazzled, every day for the rest of your working life. Look at that stretching ahead of you across the decades ... think about it for a bit ... OK, now how does the prospect of dealing with today's inbox compare?

Look, we can all do this. Yes, it's a bit more effort initially if it doesn't come naturally to you, but that's true of everything from learning to ride a bike to wrapping your head round algebra. This is just another one of those things that we can all learn – once we acknowledge the need to do it. Interestingly some of the people who are best at this are the ones who start from the worst position. I've known people with disorders[32] such as dyspraxia and ADHD – where organisation is a huge challenge in terms of the way their brains function – turn into the most organised people of all. That's because the problem has been so bad that without tackling it they'd barely be able to hold down a job effectively. So they've had no choice but to develop strategies to stay organised, and as a result they have done it brilliantly. And if they can manage it, so can the rest of us.

You haven't got time to get organised? Don't give me that excuse. Listen, do it in easy steps. Yes it will take a bit of effort, but it will be *so* worth it. Start by blocking out half an hour or so a day to get on top of things, and have some breathing space. Then deal with the inbox. Next week the diary, next the state of your desk, and so on. And then keep using that half hour a day to stay on top of it all: clear the inbox, tidy the desk, check the diary. Soon it will be habit, and you'll be calm and chilled, and so pleased with yourself.

> # IF YOU WANT TO END EVERY DAY FEELING SATISFIED RATHER THAN FRAZZLED, THIS IS THE KEY TO ACHIEVING IT

---

[32] I don't really like the term 'disorder' as people with these conditions generally function perfectly well – just differently, in ways the rest of the world isn't good at accommodating. However, in this context it seems like an apposite word to use.

Move

It's not just your body that can stiffen up if you don't move about. Your mind can get stuck in ruts – some of them can be positive ruts, but others may be filled with worry or frustration or nerves. Simply moving – physically – can give both your body and your mind a break from being stuck in the same position. So including regular moving about time in your day is important for your health.

If you work as a landscape gardener or a factory foreman or a surgeon this might come with the job. At least on the physical level. If you spend all day at a desk you'll need to make it happen. So go on – move. Aim to stand up and move around every 30 minutes through the day. You might only go to the loo, or make a coffee, or do that photocopying that isn't urgent but gives you an excuse to move about. That's all it takes. It's only a little thing. But it's easy to forget and it makes a big difference over the course of a whole day.

Try to note how often you do this at the moment. It's easy to think you move every 30 minutes only to find that sometimes you don't get out of your chair for a couple of hours at a time. Simply making it habit to move every 30 minutes could be a big change. Remember, you have to do it enough to compensate for all those long meetings where it's not an option.

And if you are a landscape gardener or a surgeon, you still need to move your mind. Physically moving can help you to do this – just have a stretch or go to the other end of the garden or the hospital or wherever you work. Switch your brain over to something else for a few moments[33] to keep it flexible. It's important for all of us to stay hydrated, so even just a minute to stop and drink some water and look around you is worthwhile.

I appreciate that there are occasions when this isn't helpful. As a writer there are times when I'm on a roll and the last thing I want

---

[33] Note to surgeons: don't do this mid-surgery.

to do is break my train of thought. When things are going well, this is fine, although if you reach a mental stopping point it's still good to pause for a few moments and stretch your legs. However if you're struggling a bit with a task often a five-minute break puts you into a frame of mind where, on your return, suddenly you find the logjam breaks and it all starts to flow again.

This is the reason it's so important you take a lunch break every day. When I'm working hard, I might take only 15 minutes to stand up, go to the kitchen, fix some food and eat it at my desk. But even that is a change for both my body and my brain. Of course the days you can also fit in a walk are even better. A whole hour off in the middle of the day is wonderful, but it's not always achievable. In some jobs it's rarely possible. If you really can't get an hour, aim for a minimum average of 30 minutes, and fit in a walk if you can, preferably in a green space rather than a polluted road. Over time, all those 30 minutes will add up to a more relaxed, restful, productive you.

> ## IT'S ONLY A LITTLE THING. BUT IT'S EASY TO FORGET AND IT MAKES A BIG DIFFERENCE OVER THE COURSE OF A WHOLE DAY

RULE 82

Take a day off

If you were ill with, let's say flu, you'd take a day off work, wouldn't you? Maybe more than a day. Your boss would understand – they'd do the same thing themselves – and you'd wait until you'd largely recovered before going back. While off sick, you'd look after yourself. You'd probably take to your bed, and you might fix yourself a hot honey and lemon drink or make up a hot water bottle. Once you were on the road to recovery you might watch some TV and eat comfort food.[34]

So what do you do on the days when you're physically fine, but mentally or emotionally really struggling? My guess is that you go into work regardless. And just as with the flu, you don't work at your best and it takes you way longer than it should to recover. You do this because it's accepted that the only reason for taking time off work is if you're physically ill.

The only exception to this is compassionate leave, for example if you've had a close bereavement. However there's a huge gap between this kind of crisis and, at the other end of the scale, feeling fine – a gap which doesn't exist where physical health is concerned, but one where emotionally you're expected to clock in and cope.

This doesn't make any sense, for you or indeed for your employer. Far more productive to get three days' good work out of you in a week, than five days of half-hearted going through the motions. So if you're taking proper care of yourself, it stands to reason that when you're really struggling it should be an option to take the odd day off to recover, just as you would with a physical illness.

You need ground rules. It's not OK to take every other day off just because you're feeling a bit below par. As with physical illness, this is something you only do if it's clear that a day or two off work

---

[34] A soft-boiled egg with toast soldiers for me please.

will make you more productive in the long run. I'm not offering you carte blanche to skive any time you're not in the mood for work.[35] This is a resource to be used sparingly and wisely; however, when you really need it you shouldn't feel guilty about occasionally focusing on your own mental health for a day or so for everyone's benefit.

If you're lucky, you'll have an enlightened boss who will understand, or you'll work for yourself. If not, you will need to make the call on how honest to be about which bit of your health is causing you to take a day off. I'd never advocate lying, but it's not difficult to be economical with the truth. You can say you're feeling really bad without specifying that it's your head and not your body that needs a bit of care and nurturing.

Even if your boss and perhaps some of your colleagues are unenlightened about the importance of looking after yourself holistically, it doesn't mean you have to follow their approach blindly. You're a grown-up, you can be responsible, and you can use this occasional mental pressure release to keep both you and your work in good shape.

> YOU SHOULDN'T FEEL GUILTY ABOUT OCCASIONALLY FOCUSING ON YOUR OWN MENTAL HEALTH FOR A DAY OR SO FOR EVERYONE'S BENEFIT

---

[35] Yes, well spotted, I'm not in charge of your life anyway – you are.

Talk

The previous Rule is important for those odd occasions when everything gets on top of you – whether the pressure is coming from work or from home. However sometimes the odd day or two won't cut it, or you start to need that downtime every couple of weeks or so. If that's the case you're into an ongoing health issue, which is a very different thing, and needs different handling if you're going to thrive.

It may be that you have had mental health problems in the past, or this may be the first time you've felt this way. You might feel that your mood is inexplicably low, or it might be obvious that it's caused by something external – family worries or work pressure. Whatever the reason, you find yourself unable to cope in the way you'd usually be able to, and going into work is making things worse for you.

You need things to change, and you can't change them alone. So you're going to need to talk to someone. We're often reluctant to do this for any number of reasons – some of us may view it as some kind of admission of weakness, others don't know how to express it, or feel that talking about it makes it more real and they're not ready for that. However, when you start to feel over-whelmed and unable to cope alone, you need to recognise that sooner or later, you'll have no choice but to tell someone. So doing it sooner only makes sense – the less entrenched your situation, the easier it should be to resolve it.

Let me stress that it doesn't matter if you're struggling in the face of a problem you can't change – a divorce or bereavement or financial struggles – because the only thing that needs to change is your response to it. The facts may not alter, but that doesn't mean you can't find a way to feel more on top of the situation.

OK, so talk. As far as work is concerned, the ideal person to talk to is your boss. They are best equipped to help you, and they need to understand why you're not performing as normal – taking more time off, or working less well, or becoming irritable with colleagues. Once they understand, they'll be able to help you by relieving some pressure, or agreeing flexible working arrangements, or changing deadlines. Your boss wants you working at your best, quite apart from their personal concern for you.

Of course, it might be that your boss just isn't approachable, or is even part of the problem. That doesn't mean you have no one to talk to however – you'll just need to find someone else. Perhaps your boss's manager, or maybe HR, or a colleague. Even someone outside work – a friend or a counsellor or therapist. They should be able to help you find a way to cope, and perhaps to tell your boss in due course. Sooner or later, however, unless you can resolve the problem without any support from work, they'll need to know. And once they do, that in itself will be a weight off your shoulders.

> SOONER OR LATER, YOU'LL HAVE NO CHOICE BUT TO TELL SOMEONE

Mind the team

You're not an island, and the way people around you behave will affect your mood. You must have experienced being part of a happy, well-functioning team or group or class, and conversely part of a cheerless or even toxic team. Of course the collective mood and ethos will have a significant impact on your own mental state. So if you want your work to be rewarding and positive, whatever you can do to foster a happy team is going to be a big help.

Your own behaviour is generally reflected back at you – that applies in all walks of life. Of course there will be the occasional outlier, who will sometimes respond to kindness with rudeness, or to calmness with anger. In general however you will reap what you sow. So if you'd like to be part of a kind, supportive, encouraging team, the best way to achieve it is to exhibit those characteristics yourself.

If you're one of a team of 20 and the other 19 are vituperative, two-faced, mean-spirited individuals, you might have an uphill struggle I grant you. However – and you won't like this – you want to be absolutely sure they're not reflecting your own behaviour back at you. It's not easy to make a stand, but if everyone becomes absorbed into the collective negative ethos, it won't change until enough people individually decide to buck the trend.

It's far more likely, however, that you're part of a team where everyone has normal ups and downs, good days and bad days, and when the pressure is on, or someone dominant is in a bad mood, the whole team can be brought down by it. This is where one person really can start to make a difference – and if that person is you, then you will reap the benefit whether everyone else joins in or not. Because people's attitude to you will start to shift, even before the ripples spread out across the rest of the team.

If you are the boss, you can make a huge difference. The same should be true in a small team. But even in a junior role in a large team you can still make your own personal experience of work happier and more positive. And, in the process, you can cheer up a few other people's day too.

All you have to do is to be kind. Polite. Say please and thank you, smile, ask after your colleagues and listen to their replies. Take an interest in them as people. Be understanding of the occasional human mistake, help out, offer support. This isn't difficult stuff.

Show appreciation – properly. Don't just say thanks, be specific, say 'You really helped me there – I'm amazed how accurate those figures were considering how fast you produced them.' There's a wealth of evidence to show that expressing gratitude makes both of you feel good. It builds your own self-esteem and gives you more of a sense of purpose. It reduces stress and makes you a better manager. So thank you for reading this Rule and for really thinking about how to look after your workmates even better.

> ALL YOU HAVE TO DO IS TO BE KIND. POLITE. SAY PLEASE AND THANK YOU, SMILE

RETIREMENT

Getting to the end of your formal working life can feel exhilarating or daunting or worrying or exciting or sad or life-enhancing or just a relief. Most probably several of these feelings simultaneously, and more besides. It's a big mile-stone, and it marks a huge change in your life. Lots of things are going to be very different, and there will be pros and cons. The trick is to make sure that the pros have the upper hand.

Your personal circumstances are going to be a big factor and, while you can't control all of them, you can control some of them. Do you live alone, or do you have a partner or family around you? Will you stay put, or are you planning to move house, or even location? How financially secure are you, and can you downsize or relocate to reduce your costs if necessary?

Control is a big part of how successfully you retire. If it feels like something thrust upon you which you're forced to comply with, you might feel powerless and vulnerable. Whereas if you can see it as an opportunity that *you* can mould to suit yourself, it's much easier to embrace it and make the most of it.

Retirement isn't a single state. You might have decades of retired life ahead of you, and the things you enjoy and are capable of at the start won't necessarily be the ones you want to do in 10, 20 or even 30 years' time. You'll change, and your life will change, as much as it does now. Look back at where you were 20 years ago – see the difference? The next 20 years can bring just as much change. So don't feel that you're stuck with the decisions you make as you move into retirement. Of course you're not. This is just another bend in the endlessly winding and flowing river of your life. The Rules that follow will help you to prepare even if retirement is years away (so no excuses for skipping this section). If it's more imminent, they'll help you to dive in and enjoy it.

Now is not forever

Your retirement is coming up, and it feels like a massive transformation is looming. You'll be leaving your workplace, your colleagues, the lifestyle you've been used to for years – maybe all your adult life. No more daily commute, no more putting on your work clothes every morning, no more full inbox, no one needing to get hold of you urgently, no one wanting your opinion or decision or judgement. It's all going to go quiet, and the most pressing items on your to-do list will be having a coffee and reading the daily paper.

Scary, huh? Even if you don't particularly enjoy your job, the prospect of throwing your life up in the air is still daunting. Yes, even if you have plans to embark on a round the world cruise the day after your leaving party, it's still a step into the unknown that can leave you feeling apprehensive.

I have a friend who recently retired from running an organisation of well over a thousand people. Everyone looked up to and admired him, needed his approval, required his permission or decision or leadership and then, abruptly, he retired and none of those people needed him any more. He no longer had authority or responsibility. He stopped feeling like an important person in the eyes of the outside world. Even if you've chosen to retire, this is still a very complex set of feelings to cope with.

I can report that this particular friend is doing well. He's naturally positive and has focused on the upsides of retirement. He got a dog and takes it for long walks every day – and he's as important to the dog as he used to be to everyone in his organisation. He's a very good example of the point of this Rule: retiring is a single event in your life, and retirement is everything that comes after it. And they're two very different things.

It's entirely possible – common even – to find the process of retiring quite traumatic, but still go on to enjoy your retirement.

Flicking the switch from 'working' to 'retired' might be stressful, and in ways you hadn't necessarily anticipated. So expect the unexpected, and try to find the process interesting even if you don't really like it. Reflect on the things you never realised you'd miss, as well as the little bonuses that surprise you. Watch yourself making the change. This gives you a level of detachment that will help you cope – it helps you to analyse and therefore process your feelings more effectively.

While you're going through this journey of discovery, never lose sight of the fact that it's a single event, and these feelings aren't going to last forever. Just as decades of marriage are a totally different thing from your wedding day, so retirement is a completely different beast from your last day at work. Any trauma you're experiencing will be relatively short-lived, and you have more freedom than you ever had before to make your life what you want it to be.

> # REFLECT ON THE THINGS YOU NEVER REALISED YOU'D MISS, AS WELL AS THE LITTLE BONUSES THAT SURPRISE YOU

You don't have to do it all at once

An old family friend was a headteacher. When he took over as head, the previous incumbent remained living close by, which made this friend's life quite tricky. Anyone new will make changes, but whenever he did so parents and students would complain to the previous head who, instead of backing his successor, would agree with them that the changes were bad news. Consequently this friend decided that when he finally came to retire, he would move right out of the area so his presence couldn't undermine his successor.

Twenty years later, he was as good as his word. He moved about 150 miles away as soon as he retired. That's a massive life change. Not only was he no longer anyone's boss, a respected pillar of the local community, but he and his wife also had to make a whole new set of friends, and find new activities to fill their time. Fortunately he went into it in a positive frame of mind, and it worked out well. However it's a massive disruption to your life, leaving work and friends and everything you know all at once.

So don't do it – unless you want to. If you relish the idea of shaking everything up at once, that's great. But there are plenty of ways to cross-fade gently into retirement rather than flick a switch. Being a headteacher isn't a job you can easily do part time. You're there or you're not. But there are lots of jobs where you can cut down hours, or reduce responsibilities, to make the change more gradually. In fact our friend who moved 150 miles when he retired bought a house opposite a school, and taught maths there part time for a few years. I imagine it helped the transition a great deal being part of a school family again.

If you don't like the idea of retiring much, then don't think of it as retirement. Think of it as a change of job and then either reduce your work slowly, or switch to another job – which might be part time, or voluntary, but which still retains a lot of the elements you enjoy: working in a team, or getting out of the house, or the routine, as well as using the skills you have. In other words, something that still feels like work – volunteering in a local charity shop, working for a small local company a couple of days a week, listening to children read in the local school.

Similarly, even if your reason for living where you do is the job, that doesn't mean you have to move away as soon as you retire. It's a lot to cope with all at once, and the move closer to your kids, or to a part of the country you love, can easily wait a year or two. What's the rush? You've got all the time in the world now, so take it at the speed that feels most comfortable.

There are so many options, and the key is to think hard about the way in which you would like to retire, before you get there. Are you a jump-in-the-deep-end of retirement sort of person, or a climb-down-the-steps-slowly type? Once you know which approach will suit you, it's much easier to plan a transition that you'll enjoy.

> IF YOU DON'T LIKE THE IDEA OF RETIRING MUCH, THEN DON'T THINK OF IT AS RETIREMENT

When the kids fly, you can too

Retirement is going to be a big change even if you do it by stages. If you do it abruptly, it's massive. As the age at which we start a family goes up, it's becoming ever more common to find that retirement coincides – at least within a couple of years – with the kids finally leaving home too. This makes any other kind of retirement look like child's play.

Remember though that, just like retirement, the kids leaving home is one single event, and won't feel the same forever. Alright, it can seem like several events as first one and then another leaves and comes back again, but when they've finished to-ing and fro-ing you'll be left with a continuous state of no-kids-at-home.

Like retirement, this can easily look like a negative. Indeed, I'm not going to pretend that it doesn't have any negatives – of course it does. But like retirement, you can turn it into a positive, whether you're single or one of a couple.

When the kids leave home around the same time you stop work, it's a huge shift in your life. Happily, however, the big positives from each work really well together, because they both give you freedom. The two biggest ties in your life until now are likely to have been work and kids. Now those ties are gone, you can do pretty much as you please. Wow! How liberating! What do you fancy doing?

If you do nothing but mope about how you miss the kids, and the sense of purpose that work gave you, you're likely to have a pretty miserable time of it. You'll probably get over it eventually, but why go through it? If you think you're going to find the transition difficult, much better to plan how you'll deal with it in advance. After all, it's not like you haven't seen this moment coming for years.

Without question, the people I see cope with this best are the ones who plan for it. They make sure they have something to occupy themselves when the time comes. I remember one (single) friend who took herself off travelling on the trip of a lifetime. This enabled her to celebrate her new-found freedom, and gave her a distraction – both from worrying before the event, and from moping when the time finally came round. Not only that, it created such an upheaval – a positive one – that she got used to being without work and kids on a daily basis while she was away. So it was much easier to come home to an empty house and a different daily routine. She had the sense to plan for her return too, and had plenty in her diary to help her settle back in.

It doesn't have to be a big adventure, of course, although some kind of enjoyable break will form a metaphorical punctuation mark, which you might find useful. A week in a quiet country cottage, or with friends you haven't seen for ages, or learning to paint, or going on a retreat – whatever works for you. Whether or not you do this, make sure you have plenty to keep you busy so you can enjoy your independence as much as the kids are learning to enjoy theirs.

> # IT'S NOT LIKE YOU HAVEN'T
> # SEEN THIS MOMENT
> # COMING FOR YEARS

Manage your family

I know a lovely woman who couldn't wait to retire, because she was struggling to find time to work. Her mother was very poorly so my friend had moved in to look after her – she could be left for a few hours but needed help with meals and bedtimes and shopping. On top of that, this friend had three children, all with kids who needed looking after so their parents could go to work. So she went from her mother to her grandchildren to her other grandchildren – you can see why she was so relieved to retire.

Now this woman was on her own and liked nothing better than looking after other people. Most of us, however, much as we may adore the grandchildren, would like a bit of free time to enjoy our liberty when we retire. The rest of the family may see your retirement as an opportunity for you to do what *they* want with your time, and not what *you* want. Hopefully there will be a good overlap here, but you risk feeling exploited unless you have some clear boundaries.

Most families aren't trying to exploit you. They just don't realise they're overstepping those boundaries unless you make it clear. In order to do that, you need clarity in your own mind about where the lines are drawn, and you need to communicate it. Do this *before* you retire, because it's so much easier than trying to explain later why you're cutting back the time you spend babysitting or caring or doing other people's shopping.

So ... where will your boundaries be? It's up to you. You can cut off all connections with your family if you like, although as a Rules player I doubt that will be your choice unless your family are abusive. But the point is that it's your time, and you're free – including guilt-free – to give as much or as little as you like to anyone else.

It might be easiest to consider how you want to spend your free time, and then fit your family's wishes around that. Are you happy to give loads of time so long as you intermittently disappear on long holidays? Or fine during the day but want evenings to yourself? Or happy to mind children but don't want to find the energy for long stretches with babies and toddlers? Or will help care for parents during the week but need a break at weekends? It's entirely your choice, and best to under-promise and offer a bit more later, rather than have to backtrack.

This is your decision, and you don't owe anyone an explanation. Don't let them pressure you. Some of the hardest people to manage can be siblings who don't pull their weight looking after mum or dad. They'll tell you how much busier their life is than yours, but that's their problem. I have a couple of friends who are genuinely happy to do the lion's share of the work because their siblings live overseas and they can see it's unavoidable. The resentment comes when you know they could perfectly well do more if they made the odd sacrifice. It takes two to allow that to happen and, although it can be hard, don't try to justify your position or they'll have you on the back foot. Just reiterate where your boundaries are and stick to them.

> YOU NEED CLARITY IN YOUR OWN MIND ABOUT WHERE THE LINES ARE DRAWN, AND YOU NEED TO COMMUNICATE IT

Redraw your relationship

If you live with a partner, retirement is going to have a big impact on your relationship. I've seen it cause disruption and even divorce, and I've seen it bring couples closer together. The way to ensure the latter is to think through the possible consequences together, and to draw up a new set of ground rules – oh, and keep it flexible because some things may not work out the way you expect. As with all good relationships, communication is going to be essential.

What will these new ground rules be? Well, that's up to you, but I can give you an idea of the areas that I've observed often need to change. Perhaps the key one is the division of labour in the house, and this is trickier if one of you hasn't been going out to work for a while.

The biggest problem I see is when the overall workload has previously been split fairly equally: one of you has gone out and earned all the money, while the other one has done everything in the house – laundry and shopping and cleaning and cooking. Between the two of you, that's a reasonable way to divide up the effort needed to keep the family unit running smoothly. When the 50 per cent money-earning share of this workload stops, the logical thing is to redistribute the other 50 per cent of the workload equally across both members of the team. And problems can arise when that doesn't happen, because if the stay-at-home member of the team is expected to carry on as before, suddenly their contribution feels really unfair. Because it is. So if you're the one retiring, you have to recognise that there will be new responsibilities at home.

However – and this is a big 'but' – the stay-at-home partner is likely to cause resentment if they think they've just acquired a junior assistant to do their bidding. No one wants to go from running a department to being told they haven't hoovered 'properly'. It's not easy handing over areas of responsibility, even if you embrace the idea of sharing your workload, but it is essential that you do hand over responsibility fully, and don't just delegate tasks. Agree between you what division of labour you think will work before you start, and then be flexible and keep reviewing. You'll need to be honest if you know you can't stand having someone else in 'your' kitchen, or if you think you're being given all the boring jobs.

You'll also need to navigate other areas such as how much time you spend together – and what you do with it – and how much privacy you each need now you're both at home most of the time. You might need to create your own spaces, or perhaps only one of you might. You don't have to have the same rules for each of you, you know, unless you want them.

It's probably easiest to make retirement work when you both retire almost simultaneously. But it's perfectly possible to make the change to a happy and successful retirement however it comes about, so long as you both make an effort to stay on the same page, and to compare notes regularly and voice any reservations as they arise. The most important thing, whether you're the one retiring or not, is to have a clear eye on the other one's point of view.

> **NO ONE WANTS TO GO FROM RUNNING A DEPARTMENT TO BEING TOLD THEY HAVEN'T HOOVERED 'PROPERLY'**

You can't do nothing

If you retire in your mid-60s, I'm going to assume you're pretty fit and active. After all, you were going out to work until yesterday. And you're still the same person – perhaps starting to get tired a bit sooner than you used to, and feeling ready for an easier life, but essentially you're no different from the working you.

Listen, you're not ready yet for a rocking chair and a rug over your knees. Now that you don't have to go to work every day you'll be full of energy, at least once you've recovered from that big leaving bash and the emotional jolt of stopping work. You can't spend the next couple of decades staring into space waiting to die. You need to keep yourself occupied and interested and interesting.

I hope you've been thinking about this for a while before retiring. You might have grand plans to travel the world, or play lots of golf, or spend loads of time with the grandchildren. If you're not looking forward to retirement, one of the reasons is likely to be that you haven't thought of anything to do with it that grabs you. So think of something – and think of it before you retire.[36] This is one of the keys to coping with the process of retiring, as well as being the way to ensure an enjoyable retirement.

You only need a plan for the next couple of years or so – there's no need to map out the rest of your life, with all its unforeseeable twists and turns. And of course you're your own man or woman now, so if it doesn't pan out as you hope, you can always modify or abandon it. Nevertheless, the plan gives you an important focus to ease you through the transition and should help you enjoy what comes after as much as possible. And who knows – if it works out well it might keep you happy for years.

If work has been pressured, it's easy to imagine that all you want to do is stay home and read the paper and watch a bit of TV.

---

[36] If you're reading this Rule in time.

But, come on, how long is that going to last before you get really bored? Sure, the first week or two might be a welcome change, and there's no harm in that if it appeals. After that though, you need something to do.

I know a bank manager who started volunteering at his local steam train attraction when he retired – I imagine he'd been wanting to do that since he was about six. I've known people finally write the book they always knew was in them. One woman I know started making jewellery. Several friends have really enjoyed volunteering at charities they feel a special affinity with. One or two have even half-accidentally started businesses that they can keep small enough not to become too demanding. Others have learnt to paint or play the piano or speak another language, or have travelled widely, or become experts in niche subjects, or created a beautiful garden, or advised small businesses in their areas of expertise from back when they had a job. See? You can do *anything*. Have fun!

> # YOU NEED TO KEEP YOURSELF OCCUPIED AND INTERESTED AND INTERESTING

Age gracefully

There was a time – still is in some cultures – when older people were seen as inherently wiser and more deserving of respect. Far too often if you live in the West, you feel that no one is interested in you once you retire. The trouble is that times move so fast now that you become out of date in terms of your language, your interests, your technological know-how, your musical taste, your general grasp of popular culture.

It's frustrating because you still have as much to give as people your age always have. Some people get to 90 without apparently accruing any wisdom, but most people learn as life goes on – Rules players certainly do, by definition – and you have a lot of useful advice you could pass on, if only they'd listen.

But they won't listen. In Western cultures at least, respect is no longer given to people simply because of their age. In many ways this is a good thing, because respect should be earned, and age doesn't automatically confer sense or wisdom. More generally, people don't tend to value advice they haven't asked for. It can sound patronising at best, and critical at worst. They nod and smile politely and then ignore it. So don't bother offering it unless it's requested.

The trick is to stay young, because that way you stay relevant. Don't panic, you don't have to share your grandchildren's musical tastes, or learn to speak street slang, or master computer coding. Staying young isn't about skills, it's about attitude. So long as you can remain open minded and interested in the world around you, you'll be fine. When you see younger people doing things differently from how they were done 'in your day',[37] don't judge them.

---

[37] I've put that phrase in inverted commas because I don't like it. Every day is your day, my day, everyone's day. When you say 'in my day' you're accepting that you're no longer relevant, and why would you do that? (Unless you use inverted commas to show you're being ironic, of course.)

Find out why things have changed and understand the logic. Worry if you hear your grandmother or grandfather coming out of your mouth (unless they were as broad-minded as you aspire to be). People may not want unsolicited advice, but they will always value a good listener. And listening to younger people – properly – will help you stay young yourself.

The sooner you start adopting this approach the better, from your 20s onwards. That's because the best way to stay young at heart is to have friends who are much younger than you. By all means spend time with all your lovely friends of your own age, but also hang out with people 20, 30, 40 years younger than you. That includes hanging out with younger members of your own family, but it's much more than that. People gravitate towards friends with their outlook and attitudes, not their chronological age – even when they have different opinions – so an open and interested and accepting approach will attract friends of all ages – not to mention that as you age and friends sadly die, there'll still be others to support and challenge and engage you. And, who knows, they might even ask for your advice.

MOST PEOPLE LEARN AS LIFE GOES ON – RULES PLAYERS CERTAINLY DO, BY DEFINITION

RULE 92

Learn to accept help

When you retire, it's easy to feel touchy about your ability to remain independent. You may be only in your 60s or 70s, but you worry people will start thinking you're in your dotage. So any suggestion that you need help can feel like an assumption that you're incapable in every way. However, if you've ever in your youth helped an older person to carry something heavy, or get upstairs, or download an app, you'll know that you didn't see them as being totally helpless and incapable and useless. You saw them as someone who needed a bit of practical assistance with a particular task. That's all.

This is about you, you know. It's *you* who might think you're incapable and useless. That's what you don't like. Of course you don't, but the answer isn't to refuse all offers of help. The answer is to think it through and recognise that we're all better at some things than others, and those things change over your lifetime. Most of us needed help getting upstairs when we were toddlers or carrying heavy things when we were pregnant or had broken a leg, or getting to grips with new technology at any age. And think of all the things you no longer need help with, like talking to strangers (that was once difficult for most of us), or driving a car, or cooking a big family meal.

There are things you're better at now than you used to be, and things you can use a hand with. Yes, yes, there are plenty of things you're better at, so think about what they are, and set them against the things you're less good at. We can improve at so many things with age, such as crosswords, keeping our temper, knowledge of vegetable growing or football or political history, not getting stressed, cooking, being a friend ... go on, you can take it from here.

As you get older, and move into your 70s and 80s, both these lists will grow. You'll need help with more things, but you'll still be improving others. So you might as well start getting better now at asking for help, and at showing gratitude, which is a skill in itself. Be genuine, and let the other person really understand what their help has meant to you. It might take only a few cheery words, but it's a valuable thing to be able to do, and now you're going to get the chance to practise and perfect it, and set a useful example to the younger generations – they'll be where you are sooner or later.

Remember that helping other people makes you feel good about yourself.[38] So if you let someone else help you, you're enabling them to feel virtuous. In a sense, that means you're helping *them*. So by accepting help, really what you're doing is *giving* help. So thinking about it ... the more help you can accept, the more you add to the sum total of human happiness. Thank you, that's kind of you.

> ## WE'RE ALL BETTER AT SOME THINGS THAN OTHERS, AND THOSE THINGS CHANGE OVER YOUR LIFETIME

---

[38] Rule 34 of *The Rules to Break* if you're interested.

Know your doctor

No one likes the physical side of getting old. No more sprinting up and down stairs, no more vaulting over gates on country walks, no more 20/20 vison or perfect hearing. You might still manage some of these in your 60s, but you'll lose them eventually. And it only takes an arthritic knee or tinnitus or diabetes to put paid to many of them quite early on.

That doesn't mean you can't still enjoy life, of course. Indeed some of us might be grateful to be relieved of any pressure to run a marathon or climb mountains or have sex five times a night (quality matters more than numbers anyway). And it's easy for most of us to find some way to stay active regardless of the aches and pains that come with age.

There will be aches and pains though, and if you let them spoil your enjoyment of life, you might as well give up now because they're not going away. They come with the territory. Some people are luckier than others but in the end, an ageing body is going to show signs of wear and tear. All the old people you know who aren't complaining about it are still feeling it. They've just found a way not to focus on it or let it get them down.

Remember the importance of language: if you refer to it routinely as 'pain' it will hurt more than if you think of it as 'discomfort'. If you tell people you're 'struggling on' you won't feel as upbeat as if you tell them you're feeling good. Your brain is listening in, and will take its cues from the way you talk about your health. And that's the trick – accept it and stay positive. It's all you can do.

However, that doesn't mean you should ignore all those symptoms. Monitor them, keep a practical eye on them, do what you can to relieve them – just don't get emotionally involved with the everyday discomfort. You have reached the age where the chances of serious ill health are starting to increase, and you need to keep on top of things. And that means becoming better acquainted with your GP's surgery. You don't have to rush down there every five minutes for every little thing – please don't – but you do need to double check on anything that seems potentially sinister. The risk of ignoring it is higher than it used to be.

Some people have always been a bit anxious about their health, and already do this. But lots of us rarely see our doctors and only if there's a pressing need. Or we like to think we're so healthy there's no need for check-ups. Or we worry about having to discuss something potentially embarrassing. Yep, none of us wants to discuss bodily functions, even with a doctor, but it's much easier to tell a doctor for example that you're peeing rather often in the night, than to go through the conversations and interventions needed to deal with late-stage prostate cancer. Your GP understands and will help you find the words – they deal with their patients' embarrassment all the time.

Even when it's easy to talk about, resist the feeling that you don't want to bother the doctor, or you don't want to know if it's serious, or it'll be fine because you've always been healthy up to now, or you don't need the check-up you're being offered. Think through the consequences of ignoring your symptoms – for you *and* for your family – and just make an appointment. If it turns out to be nothing, what have you lost?

DON'T GET EMOTIONALLY INVOLVED WITH THE EVERYDAY DISCOMFORT

RULE 94

Say what you're thinking

None of us likes thinking about our own death, but it's going to happen one day whether you like it or not. What happens after that isn't your problem, and you don't want it to be anyone else's either. However, if you haven't made any kind of preparations, you are by default setting up problems for your loved ones. The easiest way around this is to plan way in advance, before it seems real. It still feels a bit ghoulish, but it's far more manageable than leaving it until the grim reaper is knocking on the door. And what if he doesn't even knock – just barges in without a by-your-leave?

So make yourself do something about it, and then you can put it to the back of your mind. If circumstances alter, or you change your mind, you can always modify things later. But that's optional – if you don't want to think about it, you don't have to. My grandmother left instructions in her will to be buried in the churchyard of the town where she grew up. This caught the family by surprise until her sister mentioned that on a recent holiday in their childhood town, my grandmother had said to her, 'Do you know, I used to think I'd like to be buried here. Now I can't think of anything more ghastly.' If you care about your funeral arrangements, make sure someone knows.

For goodness' sake make a will, or everyone's life will be far more difficult than it needs to be, and if you're a Rules player that's not what you want. Remember that people will think the share of your estate they inherit equates to the share of love you feel for them. You might think that your daughter needs money more than your son, but if you leave her more than half, he *will* assume you loved him less. If you have a really strong reason to do this kind of thing, you need to talk it though with everyone first and make sure they understand.

Ideally though, just keep things as simple as you can. It's always easiest for everyone else when the time comes. No manipulating or game playing – just a single beneficiary, or split equally, bar the odd bequest. I know it isn't always that straightforward if there are step families and half siblings and second marriages, but always aim for simplicity and fairness. It makes drawing up the will much easier too.

It's not only your will you need to consider. When we die, our families will be stuck with all kinds of admin, so make sure someone knows where to find all the important paperwork, and that includes your passwords. Let them know where to find the box or file that contains your birth certificate, national insurance number, medical card, life insurance details – whatever you have. I had a friend who set up a building society account in a false name (back in the days when you could do that). He died suddenly, and his wife had no way of accessing the money because she had no details other than a plastic card – she didn't know the PIN number, so couldn't use it – and she couldn't prove the link between her husband and the account in a different name. Fortunately there wasn't too much money in the account, because she had no choice but to write it off.

So think about the people you care about, and make things as easy as you can for them when you go. It will be hard enough without unnecessary admin problems. All done? Good. Now off you go and enjoy your retirement.

MAKE YOURSELF DO SOMETHING ABOUT IT, AND THEN YOU CAN PUT IT TO THE BACK OF YOUR MIND

CHALLENGE

Life has its good and bad days, its ups and downs, where you bob about in the shallows, and then every so often a tidal wave hits you. Some of those tidal waves can be wonderful – falling in love, a big financial windfall, getting your dream job. And some of them can be devastating: not getting the grades to go to uni, your partner leaving you, miscarriage, a life-changing accident, someone you love dying.

When these tsunamis knock you off your feet, drag you miles off course and dump you in a wasteland, how are you going to find your way home to terra firma? How do you get back on track after this kind of terrible event, without falling over or falling apart or falling out with the people who matter to you?

This group of Rules is designed to help you to weather the storm when it comes to the really big, potentially devastating events in your life. These major events call for huge emotional reserves, and you want to be sure you're using that emotional energy in the most effective way you can. These events – some of them – have the potential to change you forever, and you want to be sure that you eventually come through them stronger and wiser. And of course that little bit better equipped to cope with the next tidal wave.

You will get through it. Look around you, and see what other people have coped with. Sadly life doesn't let many people off the hook entirely. You may never get over it, but you can survive it and go on to thrive despite it. These Rules will help you find the way.

Expect the unexpected

Of course you often have no idea when some horrible event is about to strike, but that doesn't mean it won't. You might be aware of the possibility that you'll fail your exams, or that your relationship is doomed. However some disasters come straight out of the blue, such as a stillbirth or a serious road accident. And indeed you might *not* have seen the exam crisis looming, or your partner announcing they're leaving.

Disaster can and often does strike at the most unlikely times. That's not a reason to spoil years of your life looking over your shoulder for some threat that may not even be there. On the other hand, it is a reason not to complain when it does. If things have been going smoothly enough to lull you into a false sense of security, that means you've had it better than a lot of people. So resist the urge to ask, 'Why me?' and instead ask, 'Why not me?'

I'm not saying it's your turn and you should just suck it up. The point is that feeling unfairly singled out is going to make it harder for you to cope, and a begrudging recognition that maybe it was your turn will help you to get past the railing against fate stage – which doesn't actually help – and on to the stage where you acknowledge the awfulness and get on with trying to ameliorate it.

You might indeed feel that you're the only one unlucky enough to go through this particular trauma, but think of all the people you know who escaped this, only to suffer some other crisis that you've avoided. And maybe that friend or sibling or colleague whose life is always so perfect might still be on fate's to-do list, and it's only a matter of time before they understand how it feels. I hope, however, that you'll find it in you to be happy for the people who haven't had to experience what you're going through (course you will, you're a Rules player).

Most of us have long lives, and trouble strikes at different times. I've known people who I thought had it pretty easy, only to find out that years before I met them they had a lifetime's-worth of emotional battering, or they were living with a significant problem I'd been unaware of. Comparing yourself with other people is futile and impossible anyway, and it won't help. You're here, now, and that's where you need to focus.

Disasters sometimes arrive in clusters, and that's something you should be prepared for too. Sometimes it's entirely random, and sometimes there's a connection: you fail your exams because your dad just died, or you go through a nasty divorce and then your teenager has an eating disorder – it's no one's fault, and it's often not a direct cause and effect, but there's a relationship between one crisis and the next. Again, useless to ask 'why me?' These are all ripples from the original stone that plummeted into the middle of your life, and you are absolutely not the only person this has happened to.

Some ordeals really have no upside, but you'd be surprised how many do – although they usually take a long time to show. People can go through devastating break-ups, only to find themselves subsequently in a relationship that makes them much happier. Someone who had to completely rethink their career because they didn't make the grade, ends up thanking their lucky stars they didn't end up as a doctor or lawyer or whatever it was they missed out on originally.

> YOU'RE HERE, NOW, AND
> THAT'S WHERE YOU NEED
> TO FOCUS

It is what it is

The really big life stuff changes you – you know that. The changes might be many or few, large or small, but you don't come away from it unscathed. Some things you get over, while others you only ever get through, and the reason many people resist the phrase 'get over' is precisely because it implies that things will go back to how they were. If you've lost your house or your partner has died or your child has been diagnosed with a life-threatening illness, you know things will never be the same again. Not even if you eventually get to buy another house, or remarry, or your child recovers. The reason it won't be the same is because you yourself have changed, regardless of whether your situation appears on paper to be reinstated.

You know all this, and you might well have experienced it before, but it's really important you grasp it fully when your life feels as if it's collapsing around you. And here's why – the temptation in the face of a major crisis is to fight it, to refuse to believe it, to change reality. If you're sitting comfortably reading this book[39] while life is relatively normal, it might be obvious that this is futile. When you're in the thick of it, however, it's a very typical response to refuse to accept what's happening. I repeat, *accept* what's happening ...

Yes, we've arrived at the acceptance word (it was only a matter of time). It's an emotionally charged word because it gets bandied about unhelpfully at times, and people tell you that you 'should' accept the situation when you're not ready and they have no idea how it feels. I'm on your side there. I'm not going to tell you what you should do, but I want you to understand acceptance so you can see how it works.

---

[39] Please make sure you're comfortable, or you won't be able to concentrate properly.

You've come head-to-head with disaster. You're facing off against a major crisis. And that means one of you is going to have to give. One of you has to relinquish control and fit themselves around the other. And if the crisis can't be changed – death, divorce, terminal diagnosis, financial ruin – then you'll have to be the one to adapt. And we're back to where we started ...

Acceptance means you stop fighting what you can't change, and you acknowledge that you're the one that needs to change, adapt, fit into this new world. You don't have to like it or want it – which is what makes this so hard – but you can only start to heal once you understand that the really big life stuff changes us, and we need to be willing to go through that process. That's what you're accepting: that it is what it is, and you're the one who has to change.

Now, when you're ready, you can begin to uncover the changes *you* need to make to cope with a scenario that can't be changed. And when you start to do that, you can shoulder your pack and set off, and begin the long task of getting through it.

> YOU CAN ONLY START TO HEAL ONCE YOU UNDERSTAND THAT THE REALLY BIG LIFE STUFF CHANGES US

Embrace the change

I had a friend years ago who split up from her long-term boyfriend when she was in her mid-20s. She'd never been without a serious boyfriend since her mid-teens, being one of those people who find someone new almost immediately, and so this break-up really shattered her. She was sure she wouldn't cope, and it was only a matter of time before she'd fall apart without the support of a partner. Within a couple of months she was telling me she was surprised her breakdown hadn't happened already. I think it was about six months before she started to recognise that maybe she wasn't going to melt down, and she could cope perfectly well on her own.

And this realisation changed her. Suddenly she wasn't the person she had believed she was. She was a capable grown up who could cope – even thrive – without the support of a partner. She became more confident and self-assured, and happy to wait as long as it took for another relationship. When she did get involved with someone else, she was less dependent and more ready to express her needs, because she knew she didn't have to stay unless she wanted to.

This friend's devastating break-up changed her, and changed her permanently. This is an example of how the changes you go through because of a major catastrophe are so often the silver lining. We can spend months or years refusing to accept what's happened, refusing to change, but actually those changes are often the saving grace of the disaster. They aren't always worth the price you pay for them, but they are the one real nugget you can salvage from the wreckage.

I've seen people react to big life traumas by becoming embittered or wary or brittle, but I've seen far more people emerge stronger, more self-assured, more empathetic, more flexible. Of course, sometimes I haven't seen the changes at all because they're visible only to the person themselves, and maybe to those closest to them. Doesn't mean they're not there though, just because you and I don't see them.

However awful the experience life has put you through, you can still gain this small benefit from it. Depending on what has happened, the benefit of change could even outweigh the trauma – as with my friend who gained a lifetime of confidence and self-sufficiency from the end of a relationship that didn't really make her happy anyway. And those changes are part of why the relationship she now has is so successful.

I've seen plenty of people lead apparently charmed lives, who have then gone through a crisis that has hugely increased their empathy towards other people who go through difficult experiences. So enjoy watching yourself change – you probably deserve any silver lining you can find at this point – and make sure that you're one of the many people who changes for the better. Yet another reason to stop fighting the inevitable and embrace the need to adapt.

> **THE CHANGES YOU GO THROUGH BECAUSE OF A MAJOR CATASTROPHE ARE SO OFTEN THE SILVER LINING**

Ride the shock wave

Back in the 1970s, I was working in London and my best friend at work was randomly caught up in an IRA bomb attack and killed. I had to identify his body. As you can imagine this was massively traumatic for me (although I can't begin to imagine what his family went through). Our boss gave me a few weeks off work to come to terms with it. When I felt ready, I headed back into work again on the London Underground. As I got off the train, I realised I still couldn't face it, so I crossed to the opposite platform and went home again.[40]

The fact is that some disasters take longer to get over than you can imagine, and you're not generally in the best state to judge. I'd thought I was fine when I got up in the morning, but I wasn't. You need to look after yourself, because in the end you'll recover quicker and more thoroughly if you give yourself the time you need now.

Obviously every crisis is different, and we're all different people, so it's hard to make comparisons. It's worth observing however, that very sudden and unexpected traumas are more likely to cause emotional shock, which is your brain's way of coping, and is a form of post-traumatic stress. You might feel numb or disbelieving or disconnected, or you could be angry or desperately sad, and fearful of the event repeating, or of being alone – that's just to give you an idea, it's not a comprehensive list. You could also feel tired, forgetful, shaky, sick, unable to concentrate. This will largely diminish over time, but it can take literally months in some cases.

Listen, if you have experienced something shocking, it's not surprising to find yourself in shock. You may have simply witnessed

---

[40] You might be interested to know that two minutes after I left the station on a train heading back home, a bomb went off at a bus stop on the street outside the station – just the moment I'd have been walking past it if I had carried on to work.

something – a terrible road accident for example – but the witnessing is an experience in itself and by being an observer you have become part of the event. You might not be aware at the time that you're in shock, not least because in that state it's harder to think clearly. However it helps to recognise it, because then you can look after yourself better.

So how do you do that? Well, for a start, don't push yourself. Get plenty of sleep and rest, don't isolate yourself from other people, and above all let your mind and body tell you when you're ready to get back to your normal routine. You can't operate to someone else's timetable – you just have to ride this one out. Let your emotions out, and do your best to resist quick-fixes like alcohol, which fix nothing in the long run. This is one of those times when you need to put yourself first, and let other people do the same for you.

I've seen people make choices in this state that they regret after-wards – your brain is in no state for balanced decision making – so put off making any big life decisions until you have to. For example, don't sell the house straight after your partner dies, or jack in your job. Just let it all ride for now and you can think about it later. Your health, emotional and physical, is really all that matters right now.

> IF YOU HAVE EXPERIENCED
> SOMETHING SHOCKING, IT'S
> NOT SURPRISING TO FIND
> YOURSELF IN SHOCK

There are no shortcuts

You can go through bereavement on a large or a small scale, and for any number of reasons. Some people experience it when they leave a particular job, or sell a house, or move out of an area. It also goes alongside many disasters, from a house fire to a major accident. Grief is the emotion that goes with a sense of loss – of a home, of a limb, of a loved one. It's a natural emotion that is one of the hardest of all to cope with.

One of the things that makes grief so difficult to handle is the fact that it's so incredibly personal. Even when two people appear to sustain the same loss, we have different feelings, and our mind processes the loss in different ways. So it can be a very lonely road to walk, and there's no way out but to keep going.

For most people, the deepest grief comes from losing someone close. Some people will tell you that there are four, or perhaps five, stages of grief. Or maybe seven, depending who you ask. Well, they're all talking rubbish (and it's often people who haven't experienced it who tell you this). What there are, are half a dozen or so emotions that you will probably feel at least some of, in no real order – although a couple tend to come further down the road than others. There are lots of overlaps too. And some of these feelings might pass you by entirely. The value in knowing about this is to be able to get some sense of what you're going through, and to recognise that it's normal. It's all normal, whichever bits you are and aren't doing, and in whatever order.

I've known people patiently wait for the anger to hit – because well-meaning friends have told them they're bound to feel angry – and been baffled to find that it never arrives. It's a horrible, twisty feeling that churns you up and wants to lash out everywhere. If you skip it out just be relieved because, trust me, you don't want it. If you do feel it, try to understand that the feeling itself is your own emotional response. Someone else might indeed have wronged you, but how you react is still down to you. Once you finally bring this feeling under control – which takes time – you will be one step closer to getting through this.

Another of the feelings that sometimes goes with grief is guilt. You might not feel this at all, which is great news. However if you do have a sense of guilt, it might ease you a little to recognise that lots of other people feel similarly and it's a natural response. You might feel guilty that it wasn't you, or that you should have prevented death or disaster (isn't hindsight wonderful? Obviously if you'd known that at the time, you would have done it). You might also feel guilty about ever enjoying anything or feeling happy again, as though the moment you stop grieving, you stop caring. Yep, all normal. Heart-wrenching, but normal.

So whether or not you find yourself in denial, or bargaining with fate, or depressed, is entirely individual. Just try to remember that this is all part of the path you have to tread in order to come through and out the other side. Everyone's path is different, but it *will* pass in time. You'll emerge changed and scarred, but also wiser and – eventually – ready to embrace your strange new world.

> IT'S ALL NORMAL, WHICHEVER
> BITS YOU ARE AND AREN'T
> DOING, AND IN
> WHATEVER ORDER

Forgive and don't forget

Who are you still angry with, or maybe just quietly seething about below the surface? Who is it that you don't want to let off the hook, don't want to accept their explanations, don't think deserves to be forgiven? They need to be punished for what they've done to you, or to the people you love, and you need to go on being angry or bitter or resentful towards them. Maybe your mother or father were terrible parents, perhaps your business partner cheated you, maybe your child never visits you, or your partner had an affair.

Some people hold many grudges and some have just one or two major ones. It's tempting to feel that so long as you bear a grudge, or continue to apportion blame, or keep reliving the hurt, you can keep punishing the person who has wronged you. But wait a minute, who exactly are you punishing? I'd say the person suffering most is you. Feelings of anger, bitterness, resentment ... they're no fun. They buzz around inside your head like a swarm of stinging bees. You've already been hurt enough – why do you deserve to live with this feeling too?

It's easy to resist forgiving someone because we feel that by doing so we are saying the offence didn't matter, or is forgotten. Of course it matters, and by forgiving someone you're not saying you'll forget – the expression 'forgive and forget' has a lot to answer for. The two don't in any way have to go together.

Forgiveness is ultimately about acceptance (see Rule **96**) and you're doing it for you, not for them. Once you acknowledge that you can't change the past, and that you have to find a way to live with it and adapt to it, you will feel freer and happier, which is no more than you deserve.

You don't even have to tell the other person you've forgiven them – if you ever even let them know you were angry with them. You might never have told your parents that you blame them for your unhappy childhood. On the other hand, you might have had a massive falling out with a friend over the way they treated you. But this isn't about them, so once you've forgiven them, it's up to you what you do with the information. Either way, you're not going to forget your childhood, nor trust your friend in quite the same way again. But you have accepted the past.

Personally, I learnt to forgive my mother once I saw my childhood years from her perspective. I realised she can't have been happy herself, wasn't cut out for parenthood (least of all on her own with half a dozen children), and didn't think to consider the impact her methods would have on all of us – which in fairness wasn't a thing parents thought about nearly so much in the 1950s and 60s. A bit of understanding can go a long way to accepting someone else's behaviour, without having to justify it.

So have a bit of kindness and consideration ... for yourself. Find a way to come to terms with what's happened and to leave it in the past. Not forgotten, but accepted. Close the file, and archive it safely, where you can look at it when you need to without having to rummage and ruckle and rearrange it. Aaaahhh – doesn't that feel better?

> # YOU WILL FEEL FREER AND HAPPIER, WHICH IS NO MORE THAN YOU DESERVE

THESE ARE THE RULES

This collection of Rules of Living Well joins the other titles in the series in setting out guidelines for various aspects of our lives. These are not commandments, no one is telling you that you *must* live this way. They are simply observations about the habits, attitudes and practices that happier, more successful people live by. So it follows that, if we adopt them ourselves, we too will be happier and more successful. They're not compulsory, but why wouldn't you want to join in?

How to use the Rules

It can be a bit daunting to read a book with 100 Rules for a happier more successful life. I mean, where do you start? You'll probably find you follow a few of them already, but how can you be expected to learn dozens of new Rules all at once and start putting them all into practice? Don't panic, you don't have to. Remember, you don't *have* to do anything – you're doing this because you want to. Let's keep it at a manageable level so you go on wanting to.

You can go about this any way you like, but if you want advice, here's what I recommend. Go through the book and pick out three or four Rules that you feel would make a big difference to you, or that jumped out at you when you first read them, or that seem like a good starting point for you. Write them down here:

Just work on these for a couple of weeks until they've become ingrained and you don't have to try so hard with them. They've become a habit. Great stuff, well done. Now you can repeat the exercise with a few more Rules you'd like to tackle next. Write them here:

Excellent. Now you're really making progress. Keep working through the Rules at your own pace – there's no rush. And remember, I'm not the only one who can observe other people and see what works for them that could work for me too. So when you identify a Rule I haven't included here, you can include it yourself. Keep a list of additional Rules you want to emulate and write them down:

It seems a shame to keep these new Rules to yourself, so please feel free to share them with other people. If you'd like to share them on my Facebook page I'd love to hear from you: www.facebook.com/richardtemplar.